Dedicated to
all the children of the Child Guidance Clinic
and their parents

CONTENTS

PREFACE

The topic of discipline brings to my mind a popular Tamil proverb that says, "If you cannot bend it at five, can you bend it at 50?" The proverb succinctly highlights the importance and necessity of disciplining a child when he is young and flexible so as to ensure a good outcome. It implies that it is harder to train the child the older he gets, and it becomes a nearly impossible task in adulthood.

Parenting is one of the most important and difficult tasks that adults perform in the course of their lives. One of the vital cornerstones of parenting is effective discipline. Parenting well means balancing unconditional love for the child with firm but loving discipline when the need arises. It is often trying for parents to work out a balance between these two apparently contradictory behaviours.

Individuals often learn how to be effective parents by reflecting on their own parents' approaches, researching about different parenting strategies, and attending parenting classes or discussing "tried and tested" strategies with friends. Effective parenting will lead to well-adjusted individuals; while poor parenting may result in challenging behavior across an individual's lifespan. Thus, it is important to take the task of parenting seriously, just as we take much time, thought and effort to prepare for our future careers.

I believe most of us will have a fair amount of success carrying out our parenting task. At other times, however, we will fumble and make mistakes as we try to parent our children. What is most important is that we learn and acquire knowledge about good parenting skills and put in our best effort. In the course of parenting our children, we have to discipline them even if it makes us feel uncomfortable. So, it makes good sense for parents to learn how to perform this important task effectively. The process of parenting our children is not that difficult, once we get the hang of it.

Dr Parvathy Pathy
July 2015

SPR

DR PARVATHY PATHY,
FIONA TAN, SHYON LOO

Living with

DISCIPLINE
ISSUES

Marshall Cavendish
Editions

Illustrations by Julie Davey
Series designer: Bernard Go

First published 2003 by Times Editions

This 2015 edition published by
Marshall Cavendish Editions
An imprint of Marshall Cavendish International
1 New Industrial Road, Singapore 536196

Other Marshall Cavendish Offices
Marshall Cavendish Corporation. 99 White Plains Road, Tarrytown NY 10591-9001, USA • Marshall Cavendish International (Thailand) Co Ltd. 253 Asoke, 12th Flr, Sukhumvit 21 Road, Klongtoey Nua, Wattana, Bangkok 10110, Thailand • Marshall Cavendish (Malaysia) Sdn Bhd, Times Subang, Lot 46, Subang Hi-Tech Industrial Park, Batu Tiga, 40000 Shah Alam, Selangor Darul Ehsan, Malaysia

Marshall Cavendish is a trademark of Times Publishing Limited.

National Library Board, Singapore Cataloguing-in-Publication Data
Pathy, Parvathy, author.
Living with discipline issues / Dr Parvathy Pathy, Fiona Tan, Shyon Loo; illustrations, Julie Davey. – Second edition. – Singapore: Marshall Cavendish Editions, 2015.
pages cm – (Living with)
"First published 2003 by Times Editions."
ISBN: 978-981-4634-18-2 (paperback)

1. Discipline of children. 2. Child rearing. I. Title. II. Tan, Fiona, 1983-author. III. Loo, Shyon, author. IV. Davey, Julie, illustrator. V. Series: Living with.

HQ770.4
649.64 — dc23   OCN 913323933

Printed in Singapore by Markono Print Media Pte Ltd

INTRODUCTION

With modernisation and progress, parenting has become increasingly challenging and demanding. In order to be better equipped than our parents, we have to make an effort to find out more about parenting through books and attending parenting seminars, and talking to friends or other parents who have had some measure of experience and success in their parenting.

A common topic that stirs the interest of many parents worldwide is how to discipline their children effectively.

This book, which has a mainly Asian context, hopes to give you some ideas and strategies to effectively discipline your child or teenager. It tries to take into account Asian cultural practices and values, and hopes to give an overview of what discipline is and how parents or caregivers can effectively but lovingly discipline children under their care.

It also gives specific tips on how to handle specific behavioural problems that are commonly of concern to Asian parents, as well as other concerned parents worldwide.

A chapter is devoted to the topic of child abuse as it is important that parents know what it is, so that they do not inadvertently abuse their children in the course of disciplining them.

Besides parents, other adults involved in the care and upbringing of children will benefit from reading this book. For convenience, the child is generally referred to as "he" in the book.

Happy reading and parenting!

WHAT IS DISCIPLINE?

PART 1

The word "discipline" comes from the root word "disciplinare" which means "to teach or instruct". It refers to a systematic method of teaching and nurturing our children to become competent individuals with self-control and self-direction, as well as concern and care for others.

1.1   WHO SHOULD DISCIPLINE THE CHILD?

The home and family is where a child receives his first training on how he should conduct himself successfully and correctly in society. It is where he learns appropriate social rules, values and behaviours. A child's parents play a vital role in guiding him on the right path, so it is essentially their duty and responsibility to discipline their child. By disciplining a child appropriately and showering him with a healthy dose of unconditional love, the child's parents help to lay a strong foundation for him to become a socially, spiritually and morally successful member of society.

1.2   WHEN SHOULD DISCIPLINE START?

Discipline has to begin when the child is young and more flexible in his ways. The child's parents or main caregivers should be his first disciplinarians. Other institutions such as the child's school, the state and society play a role at a later stage.

In some cases, when negative habits and traits have been formed and become firmly established, they become harder to break and the school's or state's corrective intervention can be rather painful and not as effective. This is the case with many recalcitrant, hard-core juvenile delinquents and adult criminals who frequently get into trouble with the law.

Therefore, all parents have to take their parenting responsibility seriously and learn how to exercise effective discipline when they bring up their children.

1.3   HOW DO YOU DISCIPLINE A CHILD EFFECTIVELY?

To exercise effective discipline at home, parents must know the theories and practices underlying effective discipline techniques that work on children. They must understand that effective discipline does not refer to a regimented, loveless style of punitive measures that parents employ to make their children fear and obey them.

Effective discipline combines parental firmness and consistency with parental understanding, compassion and unconditional love. Unconditional love is accepting and loving the child for who he is, and not for what he has or has not done. Unconditional parental love also means not hesitating to correct or discipline the child when he is veering off the right path.

1.4   WHAT ARE THE FEATURES OF EFFECTIVE DISCIPLINE?

Effective discipline has five important features:

- An environment where there is a positive and supportive parent-child relationship.
- An environment where there is security, safety, stability and the setting of appropriate and reasonable rules in the home.
- A strategy for systematic teaching and strengthening of desired behaviours.
- A strategy for reducing or eliminating undesired or unwanted behaviours.
- Consistency is the key to effective discipline. Inconsistent discipline often makes children feel confused, uncertain and insecure. It is also easier for children to follow rules if their parents and caregivers stick to the reasonable rules that have been set previously. Consistent parents do not give in to the child's pressure to change the reasonable rules or consequences that have previously been set.

In order for discipline to be effective, all of these components must be present.

1.5   WHY IS IT IMPORTANT TO BUILD UP A GOOD PARENT-CHILD BOND WHEN RAISING DISCIPLINED CHILDREN?

The relationship with your child takes time and effort to build up, but it is worth your every effort and will last a lifetime. The greatest test of a strong parent-child relationship will be in times of stress and crisis. It may temporarily weaken as your child grows into an adolescent and tries to forge his own identity and independence. However, if the bond is strong, it will be an anchor in your child's healthy development into an emotionally and socially well-adjusted adult.

As a parent, you will have to start building up the bond and bridges of communication with your child when he is young, as it is usually harder to do these when your child is much older. Even if you had never developed a good parent-child relationship with your child before, it is never too late. It is still possible to reach out to your child if you persevere and do not lose your patience or give up hope.

EFFECTIVE DISCIPLINE STRATEGIES

PART 2

Having looked at the key features of effective discipline, let us take a closer look at each of them.

2.1 A POSITIVE AND SUPPORTIVE PARENT-CHILD RELATIONSHIP

For our disciplinary efforts to be effective, there must exist a home environment where the child feels wanted, secure, appreciated and loved. As adults, we know that we want others to approve, appreciate and care for us and our efforts. We are more likely to try to do our best in an environment where we feel appreciated and accepted. It is the same with children. Your child is more likely to obey you when he cares about you and considers it important to obtain your approval of them and their behaviour.

A positive parent-child relationship builds up the parent-child bond and the child's sense of self-worth and self-acceptance. These positive and appropriate feelings and beliefs about himself increase the child's sense of competence and motivate him to do his best.

Successful and effective parents are parents who are loving yet show firmness when the need arises. They use effective and positive methods of discipline. These parents do not hesitate to show unconditional love to their children. At the same time, such parents do not hesitate to discipline the child when his actions warrant it, even when the disciplinary measures may be difficult and unpleasant for both the parents and the child.

Effective discipline does not require aggressive or physically and emotionally hurtful methods. At the end of the day, despite being disciplined, the child is able to realise that his parents still love him, even if they had not caved in to his unreasonable demands or if the disciplinary process had been unpleasant to him.

Effective parents set aside time and effort to build a healthy parent-child relationship, even as they employ effective disciplinary measures in the process. If a healthy and supportive parent-child relationship is so important in bringing up emotionally well-balanced and disciplined children, how can parents achieve this positive state? Let us look at some possible ways.

2.2 WAYS TO BUILD UP A POSITIVE AND SUPPORTIVE PARENT-CHILD RELATIONSHIP

There are many ways to build up a positive and supportive parent-child relationship. Let us now look at these ways.

Take Time To Talk To Your Child

Spending quality time together is essential and important in building up positive relationships with anyone. This is the first important step in building up a positive and supportive parent-child relationship.

Take time to talk warmly to your child about other things besides his schoolwork. In Singapore and Asia, academic achievement is considered very important and most children have parents who are both working. It is very common for busy parents to spend whatever little time they have with their child trying to coach him or supervise him in his schoolwork. Sometimes, busy and frustrated parents end up spending their precious little time admonishing or punishing the child for his incomplete or undone homework.

There is nothing wrong wanting to guide and supervise the child's homework. In fact, it is usually a necessary and even admirable activity in many households. However, what is equally important is that attention is given to the child's emotional needs as well. When the parent-child interaction focuses solely on academic issues, it becomes a lop-sided interaction and the child begins to think that his parents care only about his grades and achievements. The situation becomes worse when the parent and child quarrel and argue over the homework.

To avoid this, you must try to strive for a balanced interaction with your child. Continue to guide and help your child with his homework in a patient manner. However, do make time to enjoy your child's company. Your child will enjoy your company and attention and grow up happier and more socially balanced.

One effective way of communicating with children is to engage with them in their play activities. This might involve just observing your child build a tower with his Lego bricks and reflecting his feelings and play behaviors (e.g. "You look really happy stacking the bricks on top of each other"). By observing and reflecting your child's feelings and by avoiding criticism of his efforts, you are demonstrating an understanding of his feelings and an interest in what he is doing. Pleasurable activities that you can do with your child include playing board or racket games or interactive computer games.

At other times, you might want to take your child out for a meal—just him alone, without other siblings in tow, to give him individual attention. If your child likes to listen to stories, reading suitable books together might be a good idea. Again, do resist the temptation to teach your child how to read or correct his mistakes in a harsh manner.

Whatever it is, make the time together an enjoyable and interesting experience. Focus on having a nice, warm interactive time together.

Give Positive Attention And Approval

Give your child positive attention and approval regularly. For example, when your child does his homework spontaneously or when he shares his toy with a sibling willingly, praise him and validate his efforts. When your child brings home a drawing from school and shows it to you excitedly, take time to look at it and share his joy and moment of pride. These little gestures of attention and encouragement, which require minimal effort and time and no money, will eliminate the need for your child to unconsciously misbehave to get your attention.

Children who feel that they are being neglected, might misbehave in order to get attention, even if such attention is negative and in the form of nagging, scolding or a beating. This is an unconscious attempt by the child who, like adults, has an innate need for approval and attention. The child is often unaware that the motive for his misbehaviour is to get attention. Therefore, it is not right to think that such a child is being manipulative and then punish him.

Show Interest In His School And Other Activities

Demonstrating interest in your child's school and his other activities can help strengthen the parent-child relationship. Take time to talk to your child about his school, areas of interest and leisure activities. Sometimes, you can try to take part in some of your child's activities, such as playing a tennis game with him or watching him perform in a school concert.

With adolescents, this attempt to show interest in him and his activities might need to be modified, as adolescents generally prefer to do things independently. However, it is still possible to build a positive and supportive relationship with your teenager by trying to engage in activities that interest him. Again, you should avoid the tendency to correct your adolescent's "mistakes", criticise him about his choice of friends or just talk about his schoolwork and grades.

Parent-child conflicts are generally more common in adolescence when the teenager is trying to forge his own identity and independence. You might need to be more flexible with your teenager in order to help him obey the reasonable rules that you have set for him. However, be firm that your adolescent avoids negative, harmful or antisocial habits and destructive peer relationships.

With a teenager, you will have to listen more to his viewpoints and wishes, and negotiate rules and consequences. For example, your 14-year-old teenager might want to go out every week with his friends. However, you might feel that he should go out only once a month. Instead of arguing over this, both parties should discuss the matter calmly and put forward their wishes and viewpoints. A compromise can be reached whereby the teenager is allowed to go out once a fortnight. However, you should let your teenager know that he is expected to behave appropriately during his outing and keep to the time limits that you have set for him.

This style of firm but flexible parenting reduces parent-teenager conflicts and generally works better when dealing with teenagers.

Have A Consistent And Predictable Routine

A consistent and predictable routine will help your child know the family and parental expectations more clearly and abide by them. It also reduces unnecessary conflict between the parent and child. Consistency gives a child a sense of security and these secure feelings are essential for him to develop into an emotionally and socially healthy individual.

Apart from being consistent with family rules and routines, you should also set consistent consequences for your child's actions, so that he knows what will happen if he breaks them. Inconsistencies in your parenting behaviour can create emotional insecurity and confusion in your child.

Ways To Build A Positive Parent-Child Relationship

- Take time to talk to your child
- Give him positive attention and approval regularly
- Show interest in his school and other activities
- Have a consistent and predictable routine in the home

2.3   SIMPLE RULES ABOUT SETTING RULES

Let us now turn our attention to the importance of setting well-defined rules for children to follow in the home. This is an important basic requirement for effective child discipline. Without rules in place, there will be chaos in the home, office, school and in society. Reasonable rules set structure and order in our lives. It is the same for children.

Set Only A Few Good Rules

The rules that you set for your child should not be too numerous. Set only a few good rules that you think are important for your family to function well. These rules should train a child to respect himself and others around him and ensure the safety and well-being of everyone in the family. Examples include not taking things that do not belong to him without the owner's permission, informing parents if he is going to return late home from school and not hitting a sibling.

Avoid setting too many trivial rules; this can make life rigid for a child. More rules also mean more chances of a child breaking them. This can create unnecessary tension between you and your child. Focus on ensuring that your child keeps a few important and essential rules. This is better than forcing your child to keep too many unreasonable rules that he might have difficulty obeying, thus causing needless conflict and souring the parent-child relationship.

Set Reasonable Rules

Think about the rules that you want your child to follow. Take care to set rules that are appropriate for his age. For example, a 2-year-old child should not be expected to keep himself dry at night. Night-time bladder control is actually achieved at about age five in most children. To punish a 2-year-old for wetting his bed shows a lack of understanding of the normal stages of development in a child. Similarly, a 5-year-old child cannot be expected to sit still and do his homework for more than 20 minutes at a time. A 5-year-old is likely to fidget and become inattentive after about 15–20 minutes. Thus, punishing him for being inattentive after 20 minutes is unreasonable. Therefore, it is important to set rules that are appropriate for a child's age.

Review these rules as your child grows. For example, if your child had to be in bed by 9 pm whilst he was in primary school, he should not be expected to be in bed by the same time when he is age 15.

Do not blame a child if you set unreasonable rules and he fails to keep them. The golden rule about rule-setting is to remember a child's age and set age-appropriate rules.

Let Your Child Know The Rules

If you want a child to obey the rules that you have set for him, you have to let him know what they are first. Make your rules clear to your child from the start. Be decisive about the rules that you want your child to obey and the consequences that he will have to face if he does not follow the rules. If you are unsure yourself, how can you expect your child to know what you expect from him?

Be consistent about your rules and the consequences of obedience or disobedience. For example, if you have decided that washing hands after going to the toilet is a must, make this rule clear to him. Do not chide him when he doesn't do it one day and then allow him to break this rule on another occasion. If you are inconsistent about your expectations and the consequences for disobeying the rules, it can be rather confusing and difficult for the child to learn what he can or cannot do.

Set Consequences For Disobeying Rules

Once a child knows the rules that he has to obey, let him know the consequences if he disobeys them.

When a child obeys a rule, you can nurture this behavior by providing an encouraging statement. For example, if John keeps his toys away after playing with them (as he had been told), you can say, "John, you worked really hard at packing your toys away neatly. I am pleased with your behaviour. You have set a great example to your little sister." This statement acknowledges his effort to exhibit the desirable behavior, helps him develop motivation to continue his good behaviour and assists him to appreciate his own abilities.

If, on the other hand, if John shows reluctance to put away his toys, you can say, "John, if you do not keep your toys after playing with them, I will not let you play with them tomorrow. So, you can choose to put away your toys today or you can choose not to play with them tomorrow." This will send John a clear message that there is an unpleasant consequence if he disobeys and will encourage him to obey you. Once you have decided on a reasonable consequence that does not affect the child's safety, keep to it so that he knows you are serious about his behaviour.

Rules About Setting Rules

- Set only a few good rules
- Set reasonable rules
- Let your child know the rules
- Set consequences for obeying and disobeying rules

2.4   DESIRABLE AND UNDESIRABLE BEHAVIOURS

A child must know what behaviours are acceptable and unacceptable so that he does not unwittingly commit negative behaviours and gets punished. The child should know what his house rules are, what his parents accept and what they disapprove of. Again, remember to set rules and expectations that are appropriate for your child's age.

Reward Desirable Behaviours

The word "discipline" usually conjures a picture of a stern-looking person wielding a cane to stop negative behaviours. However, discipline also means the employment of procedures to notice and reward desirable behaviours so that such behaviours increase.

Some desirable behaviours may automatically occur as the child develops. For example, when a 2-year-old child learns to eat a biscuit with his fingers, his parents can encourage this behavior by praising him for his efforts. Other desirable behaviours, like good study habits and seeking permission to go out, have to be taught. Parents can help by setting an example and guiding their children through the necessary skills.

Provide encouragement to your child whenever he displays desirable behaviour. For example, when John shares his toy with his sister, you could say, "John, you are very generous for sharing your toy with your sister. This is good. I am pleased with your willingness to share." This reflection will help John give credit to himself and appreciate his abilities. It will also motivate him to repeat the positive behaviour.

Stop Undesirable Behaviours

Undesirable behaviours are behaviours which
  • place a child or others in danger,
  • ignore or go against the reasonable expectations and rules of parents,
  • ignore the rights of others,
  • go against societal rules and norms.

Examples of undesirable behaviour include stealing, keeping bad company or frequently coming home later than agreed. To tackle undesirable behaviours, immediate action is needed, especially if there is danger to the child. For example, provide the child with an explanation why the behavior is risky or undesirable (e.g. poking his finger into an electric socket) so that the child understands why he or she should not repeat that behavior.

Other behaviours may require a consistent consequence that the child does not like. These could be in the form of time-out, removal of privileges or punishment. For example, if your child hits another child during play, remove him immediately from the group and make him sit in a time-out chair for 10 minutes. Before allowing him to rejoin the group, remind him that he will be allowed to play with his friends only if he does so nicely. If your child breaks the rule again, time-out should be consistently carried out until he learns that he can play with his friends only if he does not hit them.

2.5   USING TIME-OUT AS A DISCIPLINARY TOOL

Time-out is a popular method of handling difficult, especially disruptive, behaviour in children. The aim of time-out is to teach the child a better way of keeping his emotions and impulses in check so that he and the people around him do not get hurt.

Time-out is not a punishment. It is meant to steer the child away from an unacceptable behavior. The only discomfort that the child should feel is the withdrawal of your attention.

During time-out, a child is made to leave the place of conflict and spend time alone away from others before his negative behaviour (temper tantrums, aggressiveness, etc) escalates. The child is supposed to stay in this quiet place to calm his angry emotions and stop the negative behaviour. The child is encouraged to stay there until his behavior and emotions are under control. When the child has calmed down, he is allowed to rejoin the others or continue whatever activity he wants to.

Time-out is beneficial because it also allows a frustrated parent to get away from a potentially explosive situation with his child. It is a useful technique for an overwhelmed and angry parent who might be struggling to control his emotions when he is faced with a difficult child. Sometimes, when it is difficult to enforce time-out in a child, the parent can take time-out himself in order to keep his angry emotions in check. Doing this also removes unnecessary attention on the child who might unconsciously be using his difficult behaviour to get his parents' attention.

Guidelines For Implementing Time-Out

Choose a place where your child can go during time-out. It should be away from the scene of conflict and from the attention of people. A quiet bedroom corner is a good place. For some children, it might be better to let them have time-out in an empty room if they have a tendency to play with objects in the room. Time-out should not be viewed as fun time. It should be a time and place for the child to calm down and reflect on his behaviour.

Decide on the length of time-out. Usually it should be one minute for each year of the child's age. However, if the child calms down earlier than the allotted time, he can be allowed to come out of time-out.

Explain the rationale and rules of time-out. Talk about these even before you start using time-out as a disciplinary tool.

Ensure that the place where time-out is done is safe. Make sure that there are grilles on the window and there are no dangerous objects with which the child could harm himself. Make sure that the door is not locked, if the child does not know how to unlock it.

When the child is made to take time-out, he might cry and scream at first. As time goes by, he is likely to calm down. The child should know that he is expected to stay there until he has calmed down.

If the child comes out of the room before he has calmed down, be firm with him. Quietly bring him back to the room. Tell him calmly that he will be allowed to come out of time-out only when he has calmed down. Do not shout or nag at him as it might give him unwarranted attention.

When time-out is over, do not draw attention to it by talking about it.

2.6   USING LOGICAL CONSEQUENCES

Sometimes misbehaviour can be reduced by making a child face logical consequences for his behaviour. There is no need to nag or hit the child to make him obey.

What is a logical consequence? A logical consequence is the natural outcome of a choice made, whether good or bad. A person learns that a negative consequence is the result of his own action or inaction. Letting a child learn from a logical consequence is better than hitting him to make him obey. A parent who allows a child to face a logical consequence for his misbehavior is more likely to succeed in making the child cooperate in future than an overprotective parent who rescues his child from the consequences of an action or inaction, by doing things for him and not letting him learn.

When a child is allowed to experience a logical consequence for his behaviour, he develops a sense of responsibility and self-discipline and acquires self-motivation to obey rules. The parent who is willing to let go a little, as long as the child's safety is not at stake, becomes a partner who encourages the child to develop into a responsible person.

CASE STUDY

Mingli refused to heed her mother's advice to take along an umbrella even though the sky was heavily overcast. Mrs Tan worried that her daughter would catch a dreadful cold if it rained. She worried that Mingli might be held up and would be home late. Mrs Tan worried that Mingli would not be able to complete her homework and would miss her favourite television programme if she got stuck in the rain without an umbrella.

But Mingli refused to budge. She thought that her teenage friends would laugh at her if they saw her with an umbrella. It was just not "cool". Moreover, Mingli wanted to show her mother that she was in charge.

As expected, the rain came in sheets and Mingli had to take shelter at a bus stop. It seemed that the unrelenting rain would not stop. Mingli realised to her horror that she was going to miss her favourite television programme. She whipped out her mobile phone and called home. Even though the bus stop was a distance away, Mrs Tan drove in the pouring rain to pick Mingli up. Mingli did not catch a cold and managed to watch television. She was able to complete her homework as well.

This was not the first time Mrs Tan had "rescued" Mingli. Did she help Mingli to be a responsible person? Would she always be around to rescue Mingli? By doing everything for Mingli and saving her from the negative consequences of her decision (not taking along an umbrella when it was going to rain), Mrs Tan was helping her not to take responsibility for herself.

CASE STUDY

Mrs Chan's daughter, Dawn, can sometimes be as willful as Mingli. Mrs Chan is a doting mother like Mrs Tan. But Mrs Chan knows that Dawn has to learn discipline and responsibility even if that meant she has to be firm with her.

Like Mingli, Dawn refused to take along an umbrella in spite of an impending storm. However, when it did rain cats and dogs, Mrs Chan refused to pick up Dawn from the bus stop. Dawn had to wait for the rain before going home. Consequently, she missed a television programme she wanted to watch badly. On top of that, Dawn could not complete her homework and was punished for it.

Because Mrs Chan did not rescue Dawn from the logical consequence of her behaviour (refusing to carry an umbrella), Dawn learnt quickly that there would be an unpleasant logical consequence if she did not keep to certain rules. By refusing to overprotect Dawn, Mrs Chan actually helped Dawn develop a better sense of responsibility than Mingli.

2.7   SPANKING — TO DO OR NOT TO DO?

In many cultures and for centuries, parents have often used spanking as a method of disciplining their children. Even in our modern world, spanking is a commonly used disciplinary tool. Does its frequent use make it an acceptable tool? Should we continue to use it? How do we use it sparingly, without harming the child?

Spanking refers to the act of hitting a child with an open hand on the buttocks, legs or arms with the intention of modifying his behaviour without causing injury. It is very commonly used by parents and adult caregivers to discipline children.

However, it is not an advisable method as there is a high risk of injuring the child physically and emotionally during spanking, especially if it becomes a persistent method of discipline. The line between spanking and child abuse is very thin. It is not difficult to cross the line and become an abuser of your own child.

Why Spanking Is Not A Good Method Of Discipline

Although spanking may immediately reduce or stop an undesirable behaviour, its effectiveness decreases with subsequent use. With each subsequent spanking, the ability of the spanking to stop negative behaviour becomes smaller such that a greater physical force is required to produce the same initial effect. You might have to hit the child harder to achieve the same effect as the first spanking. This practice is also becoming socially unacceptable and potentially unsafe.

Child abuse, where a child is physically injured through a deliberate adult action, can easily occur if spanking is used frequently to discipline a child. Some children have been seriously injured when their parents resorted to spanking as a regular disciplinary measure. Some unfortunate children have even tragically died. The risk is greater when the adult, who underestimates his strength, lashes out in a moment of rage.

Here are some reasons why spanking is not a good method of discipline:

- Spanking, especially if severe or chronic, can lead to problems in the parent-child relationship. The child feels ashamed, angry and resentful and has difficulty relating positively with the parent. The child begins to see the parent as an unreasonable disciplinarian.
- Spanking may cause the child to react aggressively towards the parent (in self-defence or anger). This may further aggravate the negative parent-child relationship.
- Spanking models aggressive behaviour as a solution to conflict. The child may use aggression to deal with the conflicts that he faces with his peers. This leads to significant interpersonal relationship problems with others.
- Discipline becomes harder to implement as the child grows into adolescence and can no longer be spanked because of his size.
- Studies have shown that children who were spanked harshly and frequently are more likely to grow into adults who spank their spouse, children and others when they themselves get angry.
- Spanking does not help to teach the child how to behave in a particular situation. Instead, the child's positive and appropriate behaviors should be reinforced by praise and encouragements when he demonstrates them. Such positive acknowledgments lead to a good sense of self-esteem and competence in the child.

2.8 WHAT IF I REALLY HAVE TO SPANK MY CHILD?

Spanking is not a good and effective way to regularly discipline children as there are negative effects of repeated or severe spanking.

But rarely, it might be acceptable to spank the child for extreme misbehaviour that is dangerous to himself or to others, for example, when the child repeatedly plays with fire or an electric socket. This type of spanking is called disciplinary caning and its purpose is to teach the child that a particular behavior is clearly unacceptable. In this case, caning is not intended to inflict injury and it should not result in serious injuries.

It is important to remember that if you really have to use spanking as a disciplinary measure, you do not do it in a moment of anger. If you are enraged, you might inadvertently hit your child so hard that he can become seriously injured.

Remember these points if you really have to spank your child:

- Calm down first before you administer the spanking.
- Limit the spanking to one or two strokes.
- Only hit the palm of the hand or the buttocks, as these places are relatively more padded.
- Do not use caning as a last resort as this will mean that you are feeling really desperate and your emotions of anger are likely to be at a peak. This can lead to uncontrolled spanking that can lead to serious hurt to the child.

COMMON QUESTIONS
ABOUT DISCIPLINE

Discipline helps a child to gain self-control, learn to respect the rights of others and show care for them, learn the rules of society and set worthwhile goals for himself. Discipline helps a child to work to achieve his goals without violating the rights of others.

This section answers some of the common questions about discipline as well as questions pertaining to teenagers and hyperactive children.

3.1   DISCIPLINE SOUNDS HARSH. ISN'T DISCIPLINE POTENTIALLY DANGEROUS? HAVEN'T SOME CHILDREN BEEN ABUSED AND EVEN KILLED WHEN THEY WERE HARSHLY DISCIPLINED?

Discipline is aimed at helping the child you love and care for develop into a well-balanced adult. Often, people confuse punishment with good discipline. Punishment, especially physical punishment, is one form of discipline. However, physical punishment is not to be encouraged, as it is potentially dangerous if the adult goes out of control. What we must realise is that discipline is not just the use of physical punishment to get the child to obey. There are safer and more effective ways to get the child to obey the important rules around him.

3.2   WHY DO EXPERTS OBJECT TO THE USE OF PHYSICAL PUNISHMENT AS A DISCIPLINARY METHOD?

Physical punishment can lead to serious or permanent injury or even death. Quite a number of alleged "child abuse" cases seen at the Child Guidance Clinic or the Child Protection Service in Singapore are the result of parents using harsh physical punishment to "correct" their children. These parents end up beating their children beyond what they had intended to. Besides causing physical injuries and scars, frequent and uncontrolled caning can leave emotional scars in the child.

Excessive and harsh physical punishment can cause an already difficult and angry child to become more aggressive as he learns that it is all right to hit out in anger. He then models his behavior after adult behaviour and rationalises that if an adult can beat him in anger, it is also acceptable for him to hit others if he is feeling angry with them.

Harsh physical punishment can also make a child resentful, angry and ashamed. It can adversely affect his emotional state and self-esteem. Out of chronic fear, some of these physically-hit children become timid, anxious, fearful, unassertive and inappropriately compliant.

Physical punishment should be used sparingly and only as a last resort. However, it should never be used in a moment of rage. An adult's blind rage can potentially kill a child or hurt him physically and emotionally. It is always better to use non-aggressive methods to discipline your child.

3.3   WHAT IS A GOOD WAY OF DISCIPLINE?

To discipline your child well, consider the following three guidelines:

Set Clear Rules And Expectations

For example, before your child goes out with his friends, let him know that he has to get your permission and that he has to return home within a stipulated time-frame. Without clear instructions and rules, a child will be uncertain about what is appropriate behaviour. He may then engage in unacceptable behaviour and get into trouble. The child may even claim that he did not disobey his parents, as he was unclear of the rules in the first place.

Ensure that your rules and expectations are appropriate and reasonable for the child's age. Unreasonable expectations can lead to frustration for you and your child, and can damage your relationship with him. This, in turn, might undermine a child's self-esteem, lead to feelings of inferiority and cause a child to under-achieve.

Rules for teenagers may have to be negotiated. A give-and-take approach during this rebellious age is more likely to encourage an adolescent to co-operate with you. However, some rules, such as no smoking or no drug taking, should not be negotiated.

State The Consequences For Disobeying Rules

The consequences of disobeying you should not hurt the child. However, they should be significant enough to motivate your child to keep to the rules. Once a reasonable consequence for disobeying a rule has been decided upon, enforce it when the child breaks the rule. Be decisive about carrying out the consequence. Be firm even if your child whines or pressures you to change your mind.

When the consequence for disobeying the rule is carried out, a child may show anger or displeasure. After the child's tantrum has ended and both you and the child have calmed down, tell your child calmly and patiently that you understand how he feels and that you still love him even though you have made him face the consequence of his disobedience to you. A child needs to know that his parents love him and that they disapprove only of his negative behaviour. For a young child, a hug can reassure him of your love and that you are always there even if he had expressed negative feelings towards you.

Determine The Cause Behind The Broken Rule

Finally, before meting out the consequence for breaking the rule, you must determine whether the rule was broken deliberately or accidentally. For example, if a child forgets to put his bicycle away after going out for a ride, find out whether he did it deliberately or forgot to do so in a moment of hurry or excitement. If your child was not deliberately wilful, a reminder to behave better in future is sufficient. However, if you are sure that your child defied you deliberately, you can mete out the negative consequence. Just ensure that it is not abusive to the child.

3.4   IS TOO MUCH LOVE OR, IN CONTRAST, CONDITIONAL LOVE, HARMFUL TO CHILDREN?

Love always uplifts a person. Too much love or unconditional love will not spoil a child. Spoiling a child means pampering and treating him like an emperor, and giving in to his unreasonable or harmful demands. A pampering parent does not set reasonable limits. Such a parent fails to discipline a child who has done wrong and this might eventually harm the child.

Conditional love refers to love that depends on a child doing certain things or behaving in a particular way. This creates insecurity and tension in a child as he seeks his parents' love. Conditional love can cause emotional and behavioral difficulties when the child perceives that he just cannot match up to his parents' expectations.

Children should be given unconditional love despite their faults, weaknesses and failures. Unconditional love towards a child means loving him despite his faults and misbehaviours and correcting him when there is a need.

3.5   I ALLOW MY 3-YEAR-OLD TO DO WHAT HE WANTS AS HE IS YOUNG ONLY ONCE. HOWEVER, HIS TEACHER TOLD ME TO SET LIMITS FOR HIM. WHAT DO YOU THINK?

It is true that a child should be allowed to explore the world around him, as that is his way of learning about it. However, exploring the world around him should not be done at the expense of the child's or others' well-being or safety. If we really care for our child and want him to become a socially well-adjusted and likeable person, we have to intervene when he exhibits harmful or socially negative behaviours. For example, it is natural for a 3-year-old child to grab a toy that he likes. However, it does not mean that he should be allowed to. A child has to learn early that he has to respect others. Otherwise, the child might have a lifelong problem relating appropriately and successfully to others in society.

Setting appropriate limits may not be pleasant for you or your child. However, you should have your child's long-term welfare in mind and discipline him when it is necessary. It becomes harder to correct aggressive or inappropriate behaviour when the behaviour becomes more established. Just ensure that your disciplining method is not physically punitive.

3.6   MY PARENTS WERE HARSH DISCIPLINARIANS. THEIR WORD WAS THE LAW. I GREW UP FEARFUL OF THEM AND VOWED NOT TO BRING UP MY CHILDREN THE SAME WAY. BUT I DON'T WANT TO BE A PERMISSIVE PARENT EITHER. WHAT SHOULD I DO?

There are four basic parenting styles: Authoritarian (giving orders), Permissive, (giving in to the child), Authoritative (giving directions), and Inconsistent.

The Authoritarian Parenting Style

The authoritarian parent demands absolute obedience and uses punitive methods of discipline. Authoritarian parenting results in a rigid and unloving home where a child:

- lives in fear of constant punishment,
- is not allowed to make decisions and develop his creativity,
- lives in humiliation of total parental domination.

A child brought up by authoritarian parents may grow up to be compliant towards his parents. However, he may develop bitterness or resentment towards authority, or he may become timid and dependent on others. Some children may even become more rebellious and defiant, and grow into dominating and difficult adults. When they become parents, their parenting style may follow that of their domineering parents. They may also demonstrate lower self-esteem, social incompetence and unhappiness.

The Permissive Parenting Style

The permissive parenting style is equally unhealthy. The permissive parent is lax and too liberal with his children. He allows his children to do whatever they want, even if the children's behaviours are harmful or morally or socially unacceptable. There is little supervision and monitoring of the children. Often, the children are not disciplined or corrected when they misbehave.

Permissive parents may even get indignant and angry when others, such as the school authorities, punish their child for obvious misbehaviour. Many juvenile delinquents are likely to have parents with a permissive parenting style.

Permissive parenting can cause a child to grow up ill-disciplined. Such a child is less likely to treat others with respect and concern. He may even engage in harmful antisocial acts such as taking drugs and alcohol and sexual promiscuity, as he has never been trained to control his impulses. In the end, permissive parents actually create serious problems not only for themselves but also for their children and others around them.

The Authoritative Parenting Style

The authoritative parent strives to strike a balance between setting reasonable limits and consequences, and giving unconditional love to a child. An authoritative parent showers his child with love, comfort and care and gives praises and encouragement when appropriate. He also

- understands his child and respects him as a human being,
- sets reasonable rules and expectations for his child,
- never fails to discipline his child when necessary,
- supervises and monitors his child, ensuring that he behaves well and has the right group of friends.

However, an authoritative parent is flexible and gives the child a reasonable level of independence and freedom. The authoritative parent discusses problems with the child, listens to his viewpoint and allows him to collaborate in the decision-making process involving him. However, at all times, the parent remains the final authority in the family. The parent explains the rationale for certain family rules and expectations to his child. The authoritative parenting style is the preferred parenting style, especially for teenagers. The child of an authoritative parent is more likely to grow up mentally and socially balanced and responsible.

The Inconsistent Parenting Style

Some parents demonstrate inconsistencies in their parenting style. These parents may alternate between setting firm limits and giving in on the same disciplinary issue. The child, who receives mixed signals and messages, becomes unclear of his parents' rules and expectations and is confused about what appropriate behaviors are expected of him. Uncertain about what is acceptable or unacceptable behaviour, the child might become inadvertently disobedient towards his parents.

3.7 MY 5-YEAR-OLD SON KNOWS THAT HE IS FORBIDDEN TO TOUCH CERTAIN ITEMS IN THE HOUSE. SOMETIMES, HE WILL TRY TO PUT HIS FINGER INTO THE ELECTRIC SOCKET. AS HE DOES THAT, HE WILL LOOK AT US AND SMILE EVEN THOUGH WE YELL AT HIM. I FEEL THAT HE IS DELIBERATELY TRYING TO CHALLENGE US. I AM TEMPTED TO GIVE HIM A WHACK. AM I RIGHT TO DO SO?

It does look like your child is knowingly defying you. In this instance, you have to act swiftly and decisively because his action is dangerous. Look him in the eye and tell him firmly, "Stop! Don't touch that." Do not lecture him for his misbehaviour as you might inadvertently be giving him attention. Although a lecture is negative attention, some children (especially those who do not get attention when they are quiet or well-behaved) may prefer it to not getting any attention at all. Show your child that, as the parent, you are in charge and will not condone willful defiance, especially if it is going to hurt him or others. Your child has to learn to respect you as a parent when he is young. Otherwise, it will be harder for him to respect and obey you when he grows into a teenager who is trying to exert his independence.

3.8 I FIND IT HARDER TO RESIST GIVING IN TO MY SON'S DEMANDS WHEN HE VOMITS AND CRIES HIS EYES OUT, ESPECIALLY IN PUBLIC. WHAT SHOULD I DO?

When a child throws a tantrum, it is important to examine the situation and find out the reason behind it. You may consider the following questions:

- Is he asking for something reasonable?
- Is he tired, hungry or hurting somewhere?
- Is he sick?

If your child is tired (perhaps because it is late and you have been shopping for hours) and wants to be carried, be there for him and carry him. If your child is hungry and it is near his mealtime, get some food for him. Your problem may be solved at this step.

If, however, your child has just had his second ice-cream and asks for one more and you feel he should not have another one, be firm with him, even if he cries and you feel embarrassed when everyone stares at both of you. If you are not firm, your child will learn that you will accede to his demands when he throws a tantrum in public, even if you are firm with him at home. If you persist in being firm, your child will get the message that he cannot get his way through a tantrum, regardless of the context.

If you are embarrassed and feel like giving in to your child's unreasonable demands, remind yourself that you should not, for the sake of your child's good. If your child is not physically sick, a little vomiting during a tantrum is not something to worry about.

3.9 MY TWO YOUNG CHILDREN ALWAYS QUARREL OVER THEIR TOYS EVEN THOUGH THEY EACH HAVE MORE THAN ENOUGH. SOMETIMES IT GETS SO BAD THAT I FEEL LIKE SCREAMING AT THEM AND HITTING THEM. WHAT AM I TO DO?

It is important that you keep your cool and do not lash out at your children in anger, as that can be dangerous and unpleasant for all. It also gives the children the wrong impression of how one should deal with negative emotions or interpersonal conflict.

It is best to encourage your children to share the toy or take turns to play with it. Distracting young children with other toys or activities sometimes does the trick. If these strategies do not work, tell your children calmly that if they do not co-operate, you will take away the toy. After warning the children, do as you have said so that they realise that you mean business. If both children throw a tantrum when the toy is taken way, calmly go about your work and the tantrums will stop.

Sometimes, directing your children quietly to a corner or a room to calm down might be helpful. Your children can return to you once they have calmed down. You can then talk to them about how they can better handle a similar situation in the future.

Whenever you see your children behave appropriately, praise them specifically for it. Do reflect to your children exactly what is appropriate about their behavior. You could, for example, say "Wow, you really made an effort to share the toys and play nicely with one another. You were both very kind and generous to each other." This approach will encourage your children to behave in a positive manner.

3.10 I NOTICE I CAN HANDLE MY 4-YEAR-OLD SON'S TANTRUMS IF I AM NOT TIRED AFTER A DAY'S WORK. BUT WHEN I AM VERY TIRED AND HE JUST GOES ON AND ON, I GIVE IN TO STOP HIM. HOW CAN I REMAIN FIRM?

It is not easy to handle a whining child, especially when you are very tired. But it is important that you are firm with your child and do not give in to his unreasonable demands. Otherwise, you will inadvertently encourage your child to continue with his tantrums.

One of the worst ways to parent children is to be inconsistent with love or discipline. Studies have shown that children are worse off when they have parents who are inconsistent in their disciplinary approach. These children turn out worse than children whose parents had been either authoritarian or permissive.

It would be a struggle initially to be firm when you are tired and the child is screaming away. However, if you sit it out and remain firm, your child's tantrums will subside and go away.

Sometimes, you might need to have a time-out yourself. If so, ask your spouse to take over while you go to your room to calm down. However, make sure that your spouse remains firm and calm and does not give in to your child's tantrum or hits him.

3.11 I AM USUALLY ABLE TO HANDLE MY 5-YEAR-OLD DAUGHTER'S TANTRUMS, BUT MY HUSBAND SAYS THAT I AM TOO HARSH. IN FACT, WHEN I AM FIRM WITH HER, HE WILL FEEL SORRY AND GIVE IN TO HER DEMANDS. WHAT DO YOU THINK OF THIS SITUATION?

First, ask yourself honestly if your daughter wants something reasonable. If so, then give in to her. But if she is being clearly unreasonable, be firm with her and do not give in to her demands. It is important that you and your husband agree with each other as to how to handle her. Your child will become confused if you say "no" and your husband says "yes" to her demands. If you and your husband give your child mixed messages, she will learn that all she needs to do to get her way is to play one parent off against the other.

3.12 MY 8-YEAR-OLD BOY WILL PLAY TO THE ELEVENTH HOUR, THEN TELL ME THAT HE HAS TO COMPLETE HIS SCHOOLWORK. IT IS THEN A MAD SCRAMBLE TO COMPLETE IT. OFTEN, I END UP STRESSED AND SCREAMING AT HIM. HE WILL BE CRYING ALL THE WHILE AND PRODUCES SLIPSHOD WORK THAT ANNOYS HIS TEACHER. I HATE WHAT IS HAPPENING AS I WANT TO BE A GOOD MOTHER. HOW DO I MAKE HIM DO HIS HOMEWORK ON TIME?

This is a common problem in many households. It is important that children learn to do their homework on time without stressing themselves or their parents out. Sit with your child and explain to him that you are finding it unpleasant to go through all the shouting and screaming at night. Tell him that you love and care for him and want to end the day on a happier note for both of you.

Tell your child that you want him to do his homework earlier in the day so that everyone is happier at the end of it. Suggest that after he has completed his homework for the day, he can do something that he likes, such as watching his favourite cartoon show or reading a storybook with you. Be firm about having his favourite activities come only after he has done his work. Remain firm, even if your child throws a tantrum. Set a timetable for your child such that he has time for play, rest and homework. Praise your child when he is able to complete his homework early, as that will encourage him to continue his good behaviour.

In addition, you can create a "reward programme" whereby your child gets a "star" or sticker for each task that he has completed properly. These "stars" can be collected and exchanged for more tangible rewards such as a nice book or a piece of stationery. The tangible reward should be one that the child likes. However, it should not be expensive. Eventually, the tangible rewards can be phased out and replaced with a smile, hug or praise.

It is important that before you try this behavioural programme, you must ascertain if there are other reasons for your child's reluctance to do his homework. It is possible that your child has a learning difficulty, such as dyslexia, that is affecting his ability to read and comprehend his written work. Alternatively, your child may have problems with paying attention and this may be making it extremely difficult for him to sit still and focus on his work. Children with attention deficit disorder (with or without hyperactivity) often find it difficult to sit still and focus on their homework. They are easily distracted. In addition, your child may also have worries about school or the home.

Find out the underlying reason and act accordingly. If in doubt, approach a counsellor or a child psychiatrist for help.

3.13 WHEN MY 10-YEAR-OLD DAUGHTER IS ANGRY WITH ME FOR DISCIPLINING HER, SHE YELLS, "I HATE YOU!" I FEEL HURT WHEN SHE SAYS THAT. SOMETIMES I AM TEMPTED TO GIVE IN TO HER DEMANDS. WHAT SHALL I DO WHEN SHE SAYS THIS?

It definitely hurts to hear your child say, "I hate you!" Such behaviour, if persistent, is not to be encouraged. If it is the first time, talk to your child when she has calmed down. Tell her that you understand that she is upset and angry with you for not allowing her to do what she wants. Let her know that it is all right for her to feel upset and angry about not getting her way, but it is not acceptable for her to say hurtful things to you.

Explain to your child that even when you are angry with her, you will never say hurtful things to her. Tell her that when she is angry, she can let you know how she feels and you will listen to her, provided it is not abusive and hurtful. You can suggest to your child that she can express her anger by punching a big bolster or pillow, or propose that she try to calm down by having a relaxing bath.

If your rules and the consequence you mete out for disobedience are reasonable and not abusive, you should continue to discipline her even though she may not like it. By being reasonably firm, you are helping her to learn what is socially appropriate and acceptable behavior.

3.14 I KNOW OF SOME CHILDREN WHO ARE HYPERACTIVE AND INATTENTIVE AND THIS POSE SPECIAL CHALLENGES FOR THEIR PARENTS AND TEACHERS. WHAT IS HYPERACTIVITY AND HOW DOES THIS CONDITION MAKE THEM MORE DIFFICULT TO HANDLE?

Hyperactive children do indeed pose special challenges for their caregivers. They suffer from a biological condition that is characterised by features such as hyperactivity, inattention and impulsivity.

Being restless and unable to keep still, hyperactive children are likely to receive disciplinary action when they engage in activities that require them to sit quietly, such as doing their homework or listening to their teacher in class. Due to their hyperactivity and fidgety behaviour, these children may make so much noise that they distract and annoy others around them.

Children with attention deficit disorder with hyperactivity are often impulsive and end up saying or doing what they want without thinking of the consequences. Through their impulsivity, these children might inadvertently pose a danger to themselves or others. Such children frequently get into trouble. Hyperactive and impulsive children may dash across the road or hit another child who snatches their toy away.

Hyperactive children usually have a short attention and concentration span that frequently makes it difficult for them to sit still and either start or complete their written work. Often they get into trouble at school and at home because of their difficulty with homework.

Parents and caregivers should understand that a hyperactive child's behaviour is the result of a biological condition. They should not assume that the child is deliberately being difficult.

Instead, parents should bring their hyperactive child to a paediatrician or a child psychiatrist for an evaluation and appropriate intervention. Sometimes, medication might be needed to help a child with attention deficit disorder with hyperactivity to behave appropriately and focus on his work.

3.15 HOW DO I DISCIPLINE A HYPERACTIVE CHILD, ESPECIALLY WHEN GUIDING HIM IN HIS HOMEWORK?

The basic principles mentioned earlier still apply, but you can use these additional special techniques when dealing with a hyperactive child.

Break Up Tasks Into Smaller Parts And Give Short Breaks In Between

When a hyperactive and inattentive child is given a piece of work,especially homework that requires a good amount of concentration and mental effort, he looks at it and thinks, "It's too much. I can't do it!" Finding it a struggle to focus and concentrate, the child inevitably becomes restless and inattentive.

This can annoy whoever is supervising the child's work. If the work is divided into manageable chunks that can each be completed within a shorter time interval, the child will feel less overwhelmed and more willing to give it a try.

Short breaks between periods of work will help the child focus and allow him to stretch his restless body and limbs.

Remove Distractions In The Environment

As the hyperactive and inattentive child tends to be easily distracted by all types of stimuli, make him do his schoolwork in an area that has minimal distractions. Try to seat him away from windows, doors, computers and other distracting items in the home. Preferably, the child should study in a quiet room away from the blaring television set in the living room or conversations in the kitchen. Minimise the number of items on the child's study table, as these items can easily distract the child.

Get The Child's Attention

The child often becomes distracted and daydreams in the middle of his work. If you catch the child daydreaming because of his condition, try to get hold of his attention by establishing eye contact while talking to him. Make your instructions to the child short and clear.

To ensure that your child had been listening to you, ask him to repeat your instructions. If necessary, repeat your instructions clearly and calmly to him after ensuring that you have his attention. Periodically, if he is daydreaming again, you can use non-verbal signals, such as a tap on his shoulder or on his desk, to get his attention.

Expend The Child's Extra Energy

The hyperactive child has boundless energy. As such, let him expend his extra energy in physical activities like running, once he has done his schoolwork.

Understand The Child's Condition

Remember that much of a child's hyperactive and inattentive behaviour is biologically driven and that he has a real difficulty in sitting still and concentrating, especially for a monotonous and tedious task such as doing homework. If your child finds it difficult to complete even two or three questions of a homework assignment, don't expect him to complete more at one sitting. Reduce the amount of work given to him or give him more time to complete it. However, your child still needs clear rules, firm limits and consequences for undesirable behaviour.

Look Out For Strengths And Praise Small Improvements Or Successes
Hyperactive children receive constant negative feedback for incomplete work, failures and mishaps. This can lower their self-esteem and self-confidence. It will be helpful if the child's parents and teachers pay more attention to his strengths and successes, as this makes the child feel better about what he has done, even if his work output is less than that of his peers. Positive feedback for effort helps to improve the child's self-esteem and self-confidence. This will encourage and motivate him to try harder to improve himself.

For some hyperactive and inattentive children, whose problems significantly affect their academic, interpersonal and social functioning, medication to control the troublesome symptoms might be necessary, in addition to behavioural interventions.

3.16 MY 14-YEAR-OLD TEENAGER IS DIFFICULT TO HANDLE NOW. WHEN HE WAS YOUNGER, HE WAS AN EASY-GOING AND OBEDIENT BOY. WHAT IS HAPPENING TO MY SON?

The teenage years are a challenging and turbulent period for both the teenager and his parents. What are the changes and challenges a teenager faces?

A teenager has to cope with his physical developmental and pubertal changes in addition to other stressors and challenges at home and at school. Hormonal changes, acne breakouts, facial hair, peer and romantic relationship issues, and academic stressors may make a teenager worried, awkward and grumpy. Sometimes, some teenagers become seriously depressed and suicidal.

A teenager is often adjusting to his sexual maturity. He is developing his sexual identity and experiencing growing interest in the opposite sex. These developments can cause heightened tension in the adolescent as he tries to deal with the potential complexities of a romantic relationship.

A teenager is also developing his sense of self-identity. He is trying to discover himself, his likes and dislikes, as well as his beliefs, values and ambitions in life. This is a time when the teenager can be rather abstract and idealistic, causing him to clash with adults who have alternate views and are often driven by practical issues and concerns.

A teenager is often trying to achieve independence from his family. He treasures his privacy and usually prefers the company of his friends. He has his own values, ideas and plans, and is likely to guard his independence fiercely. This might lead to conflict with his parents as he perceives them as trying to control him.

A teenager is trying to establish relationships with other teenagers and adults in his life. At the same time, he is trying to understand and control his emotions and aggressive impulses.

In the midst of all these challenges, a teenager has to cope with the stress and demands of schoolwork and co-curricular activities in school. No wonder a teenager sometimes finds the world overwhelming and becomes irritable. No wonder an easy-going, sweet-natured boy transforms into a rather difficult and challenging teenager.

Try to be understanding and patient. Your teenager is likely to pass this difficult period. However, be firm with him when the need arises. Ensure that you have a happy family, as parental conflicts and family problems add more stress for teenagers.

3.17 WHAT ARE SOME GOOD RULES OF COMMUNICATION TO USE WITH MY TEENAGER? ARE THERE PITFALLS TO AVOID?

Good communication helps to build up a relationship, while miscommunication or poor communication can damage a relationship. Good communication skills help a parent relate better to his teenager, at a time when most parent-child communication and relationship difficulties occur.

Communication is a two-way process. Problems often occur when either the listener or speaker, or both, fail to understand the content and intent of what is spoken. It is helpful if you listen non-defensively and patiently, allowing your child to share what he wants to say without interruption. It is also useful to use feedback or reflective listening when communicating with your child to help him know that you value him and his feelings, opinions and thoughts. Such a communication approach will allow both you and your child to understand each other's points of view without arguing.

Communication also involves verbal and non-verbal elements. Sometimes we say something but actually mean something else. For example, when an angry teenager tells a parent, "I hate you", he may actually mean, "I don't like you controlling me and not letting me go to the party." In this instance, the teenager does not hate his parents, but dislikes his freedom being restricted. If a parent were to misunderstand what the teenager is actually saying and reacts angrily to the teenager's outburst, the communication becomes an argument or quarrel and no one ends up hearing what needs to be really communicated. In such a situation, it would be better for a parent to acknowledge the teenager's feelings in a calm way and not get into a heated argument.

Here are some golden rules for communicating with your child or teenager:

Show Your Child Due Respect

Mutual respect and compliments are important in making a relationship thrive and grow. Treat your child with respect and avoid using hurtful or sarcastic words when you are communicating with him. Do not yell and scream at your child. A loud and angry voice does not mean better communication. Instead, try to talk calmly with your child. Take a break if you realise that you are really angry and cannot talk calmly. Talk when both of you are calm and more rational.

More importantly, avoid modeling disrespect and avoid treating your child with disrespect at home or in public. It is also important not to over-emphasise the mistake and label the child for what the child has committed (e.g. calling the child a "liar" for lying or calling the child a "thief" for taking things without permission).Instead, you should address your child's negative behavior, so that he or she understands why that particular behavior is unacceptable.

It is also important to provide credit or appropriate praise when the child does something positive. It is important for parents to make an effort to maintain realistic and manageable expectations of their child or teenager.

Listen To Your Child

Let your child talk and hear him out. Often, parents interrupt a child's conversation when he is trying to say something important. This then stops the child from communicating with his parents. Such a child might then look to other sources of support, including undesirable peers who are willing to lend him a listening and non-judgmental ear.

Understand the deeper meaning of what your child says. When a child says, "I don't want to go to school", he might be saying, "I can't cope with my Mathematics, please help me." It is extremely important to take the time to explore and clarify in order to truly understand what the adolescent or child is saying.

Avoid Confrontational And Aggressive Styles Of Discipline

Aggression begets aggression; harsh words beget harshness, and the body and spirit may get hurt in the process. Include the teenager in decision-making and rule-setting processes in the home. Keep in mind that rules and boundaries should be appropriate and reasonable. Involve your teenager in family discussions so that a reasonable compromise is reached, if necessary. This discussion process makes the family rules more acceptable to the teenager and increases his compliance. Remember that certain rules, such as no smoking or no drugs, are non-negotiable.

Avoid unnecessary arguments. If your teenager argues with you, do not get drawn into a fruitless, heated argument. Sometimes, the teenager might argue to assert his independence. For example, your 13-year-old teenager wants to attend an all-night party with questionable peers, but you have decided not to give him permission. He reacts angrily and tells you "You are mean!" Instead of arguing with him, simply tell him calmly, "I know you are upset and think that I am mean. But I cannot allow you to attend a party where there is going to be drugs and alcohol." Your teenager will get the message that there is no point arguing about clear-cut, non-negotiable issues and is likely to stay put in the house. If you find that you are getting into an explosive quarrel, take time-out.

Positive relationships between parents, caregivers and children are developed on positive interactions rather than on negative interactions.

Give Clear Instructions And Positive Messages

Mean what you say, keep your promises and set a good example. If you do not want your child to use swear words, do not swear in front of him. Do not just tell him what not to do. Instead, you have to tell him what to do and then show it, if necessary.

Give Encouragement When Your Child Does Something Right Or Puts In Effort

We all thrive on validation and encouragement. Do not hesitate to put in a positive word when your child is doing something appropriate or trying his best.

Give Constructive Feedback

When a teenager has done something wrong, do not to criticise him, especially about his appearance or character. Teenagers, who are trying to discover their identity and build self-autonomy, are especially vulnerable to criticism or rejection. It is unhealthy to employ critical, hurtful or shaming tactics on your child. Avoid using harsh comments such as, "You are useless. You will never do well. Why are you always so dumb?"

Instead, focus on what should be done and give constructive feedback. If you need to talk to your teenager about something negative, do it in private, away from his friends or others. Provide your child or teenager with suggestions to help solve his problems.

So far we have looked at the issue of discipline in bringing up our children. In the next few sections, we will look at specific and common problematic behaviours that a child may display and that will require effective disciplinary action. We will explore at how these problematic behaviours can be handled more effectively.

HANDLING TANTRUMS IN CHILDREN

PART 4

Behaviours learnt in early childhood, whether they are positive or negative, can become entrenched and become the basis for adult traits and behaviours. A demanding and unreasonable toddler is more likely to grow up into an unreasonable and difficult adult.

So, parents need to know how to effectively handle a temper tantrum before it becomes entrenched. A child's tantrums can create tension in a parent-child relationship and easily elicit negative and potentially dangerous responses from the parent.

4.1   WHAT ARE TANTRUMS?

Tantrums are episodes where the child becomes upset and goes into a state characterised by some of the following behaviours:

- Crying.
- Screaming and shouting.
- Stamping feet.
- Rolling on the floor.
- Holding the breath (this can appear frightening to the caregiver).

In more severe forms, the child may kick or throw objects and hit others around him. A tantrum can be short, lasting from 10 to 20 minutes, or it can last for several hours.

4.2   WHEN DO TANTRUMS USUALLY START?

Tantrums usually start when the child is about 12 months old, the time when he is learning to become independent, is curious about the world and wants to explore the world with all his various senses. At this stage, the child can appear to be demanding, stubborn or uncooperative.

Temper tantrums usually worsen when a child is about 2 to 3 years of age. If these tantrums are managed well, they usually lessen as the child approaches the age of 4. It is important to learn how to manage tantrums effectively at an early stage. Otherwise, a pattern of tantrums will become established and this can persist into adolescence and adulthood. Certainly, for the sake of their child's well-being, parents should help him learn to handle his frustration and anger appropriately.

4.3   WHY DO TODDLERS AND PRESCHOOLERS THROW TANTRUMS?

Children engage in temper tantrums when they are frustrated or angry. It is their way of expressing their negative angry feelings.

Children can become frustrated when
- they are not allowed to do what they want (e.g. watching cartoons past their bedtime),
- they are not given what they want (e.g. being denied having an ice-cream on a cold day),
- things do not go the way they want (e.g. the block of Lego bricks they are trying to arrange keeps falling down),
- they are unable to do a difficult task (e.g. tie their shoelaces),
- they do not know how to express what they want in words,
- they are tired or sick.

Children with difficult temperaments may be more prone to tantrums. Such temperamentally-difficult children can be rather strong-willed, more sensitive and easily irritated. They tend to struggle more with changes and are more likely to display tantrums as compared to a cheerful and placid child.

Parents who give in to their child's demands whenever he throws a tantrum are more likely to suffer the consequences. These parents might end up having to live with a demanding and difficult youngster who will eventually manipulate them through his tantrums.

Finally, a child who frequently observe adults losing their temper whenever they are unhappy or angry is more likely to display tantrums when he becomes angry or upset. This is because parents, who are their children's first role models, have not shown effective emotional management strategies.

4.4   HOW CAN I HANDLE TANTRUMS EFFECTIVELY?

Tantrums can be handled in a number of ways, depending on the reason behind the tantrums, as well as the age and temperament of the child, amongst other factors.

First, find out the reason for your child's tantrum. Your child may be distressed, tired or scared. A comforting hug, some reassuring words or a nap may be enough to soothe him. If your child is having a temper tantrum in public, you can excuse yourself from the situation or place and go home. More importantly, you should avoid giving the temper tantrum undue attention, either positively or negatively.

If the tantrum happens because the child is not allowed to do what he wants, such as playing with a toy that his brother is playing with, you can distract him by showing him another toy.

Sometimes, reasoning may help to calm a child who is throwing a tantrum. You may want to reflect your child's feelings of anger or disappointment. This will help your child see that you understand how he is feeling. This feeling of being understood, by itself, may calm your child down. For example, you could say to the child, "It looks like you are angry (with Sue for not giving you the toy). Tell me more about it." With this, you are helping your child to become aware of his angry feelings, label his feelings correctly and express them appropriately through words rather than through negative, aggressive actions. Even adults feel better when someone takes the time to listen to their grouses. It is the same with children.

If you are sure that your child is being unreasonable and is throwing a tantrum just to get his way, keep your cool and calmly ignore him until he stops crying. If your child's tantrum persists, you can lead him quietly to a corner to cool down. As you do so, tell your child calmly that he can rejoin his friends when he has calmed down.

Do not shout at your child or call him names such as "stupid" or "cry-baby", as that may anger and hurt him, and aggravate the situation. Having a time-out room, where your child can calm down on his own, may help.

4.5   CAN TANTRUMS BE PREVENTED?

Sometimes tantrums can be prevented or stopped before they become full-blown. It may be helpful to identify the triggers that set off your child's temper tantrum. You can do this by observing what is happening before the child's temper tantrum is triggered and trying new things to avoid the triggers. You can then teach your child to recognise what makes him have a tantrum and help him deal with the triggers in a more acceptable way.

For example, a young child who is trying to pull out an electric cord out of curiosity may throw a tantrum when he is stopped from doing so. To prevent a tantrum in such a situation, the child's parents should keep the electrical object out of his reach and sight. Doing so will minimise the number of times they will have to say, "No!" or "Don't touch it!" to the child. It reduces unnecessary parent-child conflicts at an age where a child is trying to be independent and testing his parent's limits.

Another way of averting a tantrum is to divert the child's attention to an interesting toy or engage him in another interesting activity.

A child who is a perfectionist may lose his temper more easily. He may become frustrated when he tries to do something difficult and cannot get it right. You can help such a child by setting realistic expectations and giving him tasks that are within his ability.

For example, if your child is not able to tie his shoelaces and gets frustrated when trying to tie them, let him use shoes with Velcro fasteners instead. You can also tell your child that you too had difficulty tying your shoelaces when you were his age and that eventually you succeeded. Sharing your own experiences with similar difficulties is better than calling your child names or belittling him.

Or, if your child is not yet ready to handle colour pencils to colour his pictures, get him large crayons that his tiny hands can hold, as this will help to minimise his frustration and sense of failure. You can also gently encourage your child by explaining to him that it is all right to fail sometimes and that we all can learn from our mistakes. Praise your child for the efforts he makes, rather than for the completed work, especially if he is sensitive to failures and criticisms.

If you realise that your child is throwing a tantrum because he feels neglected or is anxious about something, address the underlying cause. The tantrums may abate when the underlying issues are identified and correctly tackled. This approach means taking the time to talk and play with your child. It means avoiding purely focusing on your child's academic work and looking seriously into his emotional needs for love, acceptance and attention.

Key Points in Managing Tantrums
- Plan ahead to prevent tantrums
- Give attention and praise when your child behaves well
- Ignore your child when he throws a tantrum, but ensure that everyone's safety is not compromised
- Tell your child what you want him to do and use time-out if he continues to throw a tantrum
- Let him rejoin the activity once his tantrum stops and avoid nagging him about the incident

OVERCOMING HOMEWORK WOES

PART 5

Quite commonly, parents find it difficult to get their children to do their homework. Consequently, the parents get stressed out and exasperated. Instead of experiencing joy in their relationship with their children and spending quality time with them, parents feel that their home has become a place where battles are constantly fought over homework. In such a home, it can be extremely difficult for parents build a meaningful relationship with their child.

Quite often, when a parent feels frustrated and helpless about a child's refusal to do homework, he might resort to physical discipline, such as caning or hitting the child. These acts can easily turn abusive. Child abuse cases may be caused by a parent hitting the child for not doing schoolwork. In most cases, the parents love and care for their children. However, they hit their child thinking (wrongly) that this method of discipline will work.

Usually, these parents harbour no intention of abusing their children. Most of these parents mean well. However, they end up hurting their children as they do not know how to handle the "homework battles" with their children without resorting to physical methods such as hitting and caning.

Doing homework should not be a time of stress and pressure for the child or the parent. Homework time should be a time where a parent provides encouragement to a child and helps him with his homework, if it is required. It is an opportunity for a child to improve his understanding of his schoolwork and get help if he cannot.

So, how can we help our children develop the discipline and self-motivation to do their homework?

5.1   WHY DO CHILDREN HAVE DIFFICULTIES DOING THEIR HOMEWORK?

Before we can effectively help a child to do his homework, we need to know the reasons why he may be refusing to do the work. Let us look at some common reasons for a child to refuse doing his homework.

Inability To Do The Work

Although a child's homework is usually based on what he has been taught during his lessons in class, there will be times when he simply does not know how to do the assignment. As adults, we too have faced this situation in our work or school lives.

Learning Difficulties

Some children may have learning difficulties, such as mild, moderate or severe reading difficulties, or difficulties in spelling, writing or mathematics. Some children might have mental retardation or IQ difficulties. Refusing to do homework may be a child's way of coping with this difficulty or his fear of failure. This problem may be more marked in a child who is sensitive to failure and for whom academic achievement is important, especially if he perceives that his parents' approval or acceptance of him depends on his academic grades.

Poor Time Management Skills

Some children may not begin or complete their homework because of poor time management skills. These children tend to put off their homework until the last minute and then rush through it.

Homework Is Boring

Some children find homework a boring chore and prefer to spend their time doing more interesting things like playing computer games or watching television. The problem gets worse when they have little parental supervision or when their parents are unable to exert reasonable control over them.

The Child With Attention Deficit Disorder With Or Without Hyperactivity

Children with attention deficit disorder with or without hyperactivity often have serious attention difficulties that makes it rather difficult for them to sit still and focus or concentrate on their homework. They have problem starting their homework, get easily distracted or become dreamy and lose their ability to concentrate on their homework. Many of them find sitting still and focusing on their homework a boring and rather tedious chore. They are often disorganised.

As a result of their biologically driven inattentiveness and lack of focus during their lessons at school, they may not know how to do their written assignment. Because of their inattention, it is not uncommon for such a child to be reluctant to do his homework.

The Neglected Or Troubled Child

Occasionally, there are some children who will not do their homework without a fuss as they are used to getting attention by being tardy about it. These children may be feeling neglected by their parents. For such children, getting negative attention, in the form of a scolding or nagging, is preferable to not being noticed when they complete their homework without a fuss.

Some children may be troubled by things at home (parental quarrels, parental divorce or sickness, physical or sexual abuse) or at school (bullying) and may not feel like doing schoolwork because they are depressed and cannot concentrate on their work. Again, these are unconscious processes. The child did not knowingly plan to get negative attention through his tardiness about homework.

5.2 HOW CAN WE GET CHILDREN TO DO THEIR HOMEWORK WITH LESS STRESS?

Give them time to unwind after school

Just as adults need to unwind after a hard day's work in the office, a child also needs a break after returning from school. Let your child take his meal and rest for a short while before you ask him to start on his homework. To a child, schoolwork is hard work.

Set Aside Time And A Place For Homework

Draw up a schedule for daily work. Homework should begin after your child has rested. Homework should preferably be tackled before other activities, like playing or watching television.

Tell your child clearly that he can watch television or play only after he has completed a reasonable portion of his homework to the best of his ability. Be firm about this rule even if your child whines or throws a tantrum. If your child refuses to do his homework and switches on the television, you have to take charge. Switch off the television so that your child gets a clear message that you mean what you say.

When he starts doing his homework, praise him for obeying you. After he has completed his homework, you can let him play or watch his favourite show.

Set aside a place for your child to do his homework, preferably somewhere quiet where there is minimal distraction (usually an area away from the living room where the main family activities are carried out). This is especially important if your child has a short attention span.

Praise Your Child's Efforts

A child may need to have you close by to help him with his homework. Encourage your child to try to do the work himself first, before giving him the answers. Praise him for the effort he puts in, rather than focusing on the end results.

For example, if your child is trying to spell the word "hippopotamus" and he spells it as "hippotamas", praise him for getting some of the letters right and then show him how the word should be spelt. Do not criticise, shame or shout at him for making mistakes. Such behaviours only serve to discourage your child. Furthermore, your child will begin to associate doing homework with unpleasant encounters with his parents.

Offer Some Form Of Reward

Reward your child for doing his homework. Although it would be better for a child to do his homework for the intrinsic benefit of doing it (that is, for an understanding of the topic which is then translated into good grades), some children, especially the younger ones, often need to have tangible rewards first to motivate them to do their homework.

The rewards can vary from child to child. Choose a reward that is feasible, so that you can keep your promise to your child. After your child has completed a particular piece of work, praise him and give him what you had promised. If you break your promise, your child will lose his trust in you and may not co-operate in future.

Depending on the child's age, you can divide the homework and the time to do it into blocks of either 30 or 45 minutes. When a piece of homework is completed well, praise your child and reward him with one point, a star or a sticker. After a short break, he can work on another block of homework for the next 30 or 45 minutes and get another point, star or sticker. Remember that the reward should be given for the effort your child puts into doing his homework, rather than for getting all the answers correct (as he may not always be able to give all the correct answers). Alternatively, your child can accumulate his points and collect his reward, at the end of the week.

Just make sure that your child does not get the anticipated reward before he has completed the expected task. You will need the co-operation of other family members to ensure that your child does not get these pre-determined rewards from them without your knowledge. That will destroy his motivation.

Whatever the task is, make sure that the expectations you set out for a child are reasonable. For example, a 6-year-old child should not be expected to sit for longer than 20 minutes. If your child has a big pile of work to do from school, he should be expected to complete just that for the day, in order to receive his reward. It would be unreasonable to expect your child to do his schoolwork and his tuition work all in one night. Your child needs time to have fun and rest, if he is to function well as a student.

A child who is able to sit through and do most of his homework at one go can be rewarded with a treat (for example, an hour of television later or on weekends) instead of a star or sticker, after he has completed his work. When your child has developed the habit of doing his homework routinely with minimal reminders, continue to motivate him with praise, approval and occasional material rewards.

Ensure A Happy Family Environment

Give your child lots of love, care and attention. Balance this with firm but loving discipline. A happy child is more likely to be able to concentrate on his work.

Ensure that you and your spouse have a good marriage. Even if there are conflicts in your marriage, try to resolve them in healthy ways. A significant number of children do poorly in school or under-achieve when they are continually witnessing quarrels between their parents and worrying that their parents might either injure each other or split up.

Keep The Channels Of Communication Open

Make time to communicate with your child regularly about the things that are important or interesting to him. Remember that talking to your child and communicating with him is a two-way process. You have to listen to your child's feelings, ideas, opinions and experiences.

As you listen to your child, show him that you understand what he is saying by paying attention to him and saying words such as "Oh, is that so? It looks like you feel sad about what happened." This will encourage him to share with you more about what is going on in his life and his feelings. It will also communicate to your child that you value him and care for him. Such positive interactions will enhance your relationship with your child and encourage him to obey you.

Sometimes, active listening may mean keeping silent and letting your child talk. Do not interrupt and minimise his feelings or experiences by saying things such as "Oh, no, how can you be so stupid to make that mistake?" Such a comment will hurt him (when his ego has already been bruised) and discourage him from talking to you further. The next time, when you try to talk to him, your child might just say, "No, everything is okay", when he is actually hurting inside and wishing for someone to talk to.

5.3   WHAT ARE THE LEARNING, EMOTIONAL OR PSYCHOLOGICAL PROBLEMS THAT A CHILD MAY HAVE?

Sometimes a child has difficulty doing his homework because of underlying learning, emotional or psychological problems. You will need to get professional help for these problems.

Children with attention deficit disorder (with or without hyperactivity) find it difficult to sit still and pay attention to their work. They are impulsive and easily distracted. Parents and teachers of such children often complain that these children have difficulty getting started on their homework or completing their homework. These children need to learn certain behavioural techniques or even use medication to help them do their work.

Some children may have learning difficulties that cause them to display problems during homework time. These may be reading, spelling, writing or arithmetic difficulties. If you suspect that your child has a learning difficulty, arrange for him to be tested and get appropriate help. There are specialist teachers and professionals in the school and community who can help your child.

A child's ability to concentrate on his homework can also be hindered by his emotional state. For example, if a child's parents frequently fight at home, the child will not be able to concentrate and focus on his schoolwork because his mind is full of worries about his parents or himself. A worried mind and wounded spirit cannot function efficiently.

There are also children who struggle with their homework because they have undiagnosed mild to moderate mental retardation. These children find the normal school curriculum difficult to follow and therefore display problems connected with doing homework. Such children will need an easier curriculum that is specifically tailored to their needs and capabilities.

To be fair to a child, it is important that these underlying conditions are recognised and treated accordingly.

5.4   WHAT IF MY CHILD REFUSES TO CO-OPERATE AND COMPLETE HIS SCHOOLWORK?

If your child refuses to co-operate, let him face the logical consequences of his inaction. Facing up to the logical consequences for his misbehavior helps a child learn that he is accountable for his actions, without damaging his self-esteem. For example, if your child does not do his homework as expected, he should not be allowed to watch his favourite TV show or play computer games. It is as simple as that, no arguments or negotiations. The reward has to come after the agreed task has been completed and not before. If not, there is no reward.

Here is another example of a logical consequence. A child who does not complete his homework will have to face the consequences at school the next day. He might be made to stay in during recess or after school to complete his homework. A parent should not rescue the child by doing his homework for him or writing a letter to the teacher to excuse him. Neither should he rush off to confront the child's teacher.

Effective Homework Strategies
- Give your child time to unwind first
- Set aside some time for him do his homework
- Set aside a place to do homework
- Reward the child for doing homework
- Make use of logical consequences
- Ensure the family environment is happy, loving and safe
- Look out for other underlying learning, emotional or psychological problems that could contribute to learning problems

HANDLING FIGHTS AND
AGGRESSION IN CHILDREN

A common scenario where a parent has to quickly step in and enforce effective discipline in the home is when siblings fight. It is a common complaint of parents seeking help for their child's behavioural problems. It is also a common cause for parental stress in the home.

6.1   WHY DO CHILDREN FIGHT?

Like adults, children get involved in fights with one another when they are unhappy and disagree about something. Fighting is not to be encouraged as children can get hurt, sometimes badly. If left unchecked, fighting can become a serious problem for the child and others around him, and persist into adolescence and adulthood. Children have to learn to resolve their conflicts in non-aggressive ways.

Some of the reasons children usually fight include the following:

- Things do not go the way they want and they get angry and frustrated.
- They do not know how to resolve conflicts peacefully.
- They are jealous or competitive, especially with siblings.
- They get what they want when they are aggressive.
- They learn from observing others (parents and friends) that aggression gets them what they want or is the "right" way to express their anger and frustration.

6.2   HOW CAN PARENTS ENCOURAGE THEIR CHILD TO PLAY CO-OPERATIVELY?

This is best taught in the context of peer or sibling relationships where a child has the opportunity to practise the social skills that his parents have taught him.

Explain The Rules

Tell your child that he is expected to play nicely and co-operatively with his friends and siblings. This means that he has to follow simple rules such as sharing his toys, taking turns at play, asking for permission to play with a toy that does not belong to him, and not hitting another child. Explain to your child the benefits of playing co-operatively with his friends.

Create Opportunities For Interaction

Children need opportunities to interact with their peers in order to develop good social skills. You need to create these opportunities. To help your child, you can role-play some of the social skills that he will need to use with his peers or friends. For example, when you play a board game with him, show him how to wait for his turn and be courteous. Show him how to handle his disappointment if he loses the game.

Give Praise For Positive Behaviours

Praise your child when you see him playing well with his friends or siblings. You may want to reward him with stickers or snacks in the initial stages.

Show Ways To Solve Problems

It is helpful to show your child how to resolve conflicts and problems when he plays with his friends. When you see your child grab his friend's toy, you can tell him, "Johnny, ask Anne nicely to let you play with the ball". Or, if your child is getting upset with another child for hogging the swing and is showing his frustration, you can tell him, "Johnny, tell Sharon politely but firmly that it is your turn now to play." If both of them insist on playing on the swing, suggest that they throw a die to decide who goes first instead of fighting over it. Encourage children to take turns and follow appropriate rules for the games that they play. When the children take your advice and play amicably, praise them for resolving their conflict in a friendly way.

Set A Good Example Yourself

Show a child how you resolve conflicts with others (your spouse, children, and neighbours) in a positive way, for example, through negotiation, listening and compromise. Do not expect your child to resolve his conflicts in a non-aggressive way if you yourself do not set a good example.

Encouraging Co-Operative Play In Your Child

- Explain the rules
- Create opportunities to interact with others
- Give appropriate praise for positive behaviours
- Show your child how to solve problems
- Set a good example yourself

DEALING WITH CHILDREN WHO LIE

When children tell lies, parents and other adults get upset about it and want to discipline them. Lying affects a parent's opinion of a child and his ability to trust the child, and trust is important in a parent-child relationship. Lying also affects how a child's friends and peers view him.

If lying is allowed to persist in a child, it can become a bad habit that can have harmful consequences for the child and others around him. As such, it is important to know what to do when a child is caught lying.

7.1   WHY DO CHILDREN TELL LIES?

Telling untrue stories sometimes happen among preschoolers who are operating at the preoperational stage characterised by egocentric (self-centred), concrete and "magical" thinking.

This is the age when teddy bears can talk (the child actually believes this, which is why storybook characters like Winnie the Pooh and the Three Little Pigs are popular among preschoolers and young children). These preschool children may mix fantasy with reality and tell stories without deliberately intending to lie or cheat.

However, as a child approaches school age, he is able to see the difference between fantasy and reality and stops spinning tall stories. He also gradually develops moral values and understands that lying is wrong, elicits punishment and can incur the wrath and disapproval of his parents and others.

Lying becomes a problem if it persists even when a child no longer has "magical" thinking and knows that he is not telling the truth, and lies to manipulate or deceive others.

A child may lie for the following reasons:
- To avoid the consequences of doing something that others disapprove of or forbid (e.g. lying that he did not have a cold drink as he knows that it is forbidden).
- To avoid punishment for doing something wrong (e.g. lying that he did not break a prized ornamental vase for fear of getting punished).
- To avoid doing something which he does not enjoy (e.g. lying that there is no homework so that he can escape from the mundane task and do something he likes instead, like watching television).
- If he benefits from lying (e.g. if he escapes from being punished when he lies that he did not break the expensive vase).

- If he tells the truth and is punished for it (e.g. he admits that he broke the vase and is caned, instead of being praised for being honest).
- if lying is seen to be acceptable (e.g. if a child witnesses his parents or other adults lying and getting away with it or benefiting from it, he might model after them. Thus, parents who tell white lies set a bad example for their children.)
- To unconsciously get attention and approval (e.g. lying about what he has done or what he can do. Such boastful lying is more likely to be told if a child has a low self-esteem and is bored or lonely.)
- To "protect" another person (e.g. lying to a girlfriend that her hairdo is pretty so as not to hurt her feelings).

7.2   WHAT SHOULD I DO IF MY CHILD LIES?

Discuss Your Concern About His Lying

Explain to your child that lying is unacceptable and that you want him to stop lying. Tell him that you get upset, disappointed and sad when he lies. Let him know how his lies makes you and others lose trust in his words.

It is important that you tell your child all these in a calm manner so that he is really able to listen to what you have to say. Shouting at your child can drown out your concern and make him angry and defensive.

Find Out The Reason Behind The Lie

Most children will not tell you their reason for lying. Sometimes, they themselves are not fully aware why they had lied in the first place. Even then, it is useful to find out the underlying cause so that you can help your child deal with it.

Perhaps your child lied about his homework because he did not know how to do it and was afraid to ask you for help. In this instance, you can reassure your child that all that you want him to do is to try his best. Reassure him that you would not punish him for not knowing how to do his homework as long as he had tried his best. Keep your word to him.

Sometimes a child might try to defend himself and argue his way out. Do not get into an argument with him. Just state calmly that you want him to tell the truth from then on.

Have A Consequence For Lying

If your child lies, let him face a consequence that is unpleasant and that would deter him from lying. Deal with the lying before dealing with the problem that caused your child to lie. Mete out consequences for both.

These consequences can involve loss of an activity or privilege. If your child lied that he did not break the vase so that he could escape punishment, you can withdraw an activity that he had been looking forward to. For example, an outing to the beach. Then, provide another consequence for breaking the vase, such as deducting money from his piggy bank to pay for a new vase.

Praise a child when he is honest and does not lie. For example, if your child had taken the cookies from the cookie jar despite being forbidden, and he admits to it when confronted, praise him for being honest first and then explain why you had restricted him from having too many cookies (for example, you can state that the cookies will ruin his appetite for dinner).

You might want to draw up a contract where your child could gain reward points for telling the truth and be fined a small sum (for example, 10 cents) each time he is caught lying.

HANDLING STEALING IN CHILDREN

PART 8

Stealing is unacceptable at any age, especially if it becomes a repeated or chronic pattern of behaviour. Stealing ignores the rights of others and eventually backfires on the person who steals — when people around the child find out, they will have a negative opinion of him and tend to distrust him in the future. Therefore, it is important for parents to know how to handle and help a child who steals.

8.1   WHY DO CHILDREN STEAL?

Let us look at some common reasons for a child to steal.

A perceived want or simply out of greed

A child may see a toy or a wallet with money and want it so much that he yields to temptation and takes it. Or, he might steal something he needs because he cannot afford to buy it.

Peer Pressure

This usually happens when a child goes out in a group and is encouraged to steal something from a shop. Some children may give in to peer pressure when challenged to a dare and this is more likely for a child who has low self-esteem and a greater need for peer acceptance. Parents have to emphasise to the child the need to say "No" when his peers tempt him to steal. It does not help when a parent excuses a child who steals and blames his friends instead. Instead, the parent can discuss with the child how he can effectively handle negative peer pressure and temptations in the future.

Underlying Emotional Difficulties

There are examples in life where responsible and law-abiding adults have shoplifted because of stress or depression. Children who are stressed or worried about personal or family issues may steal as a way of coping with their negative feelings.

Perceived Neglect By One's Parents

A child may steal once and discover that his action elicits a response from his parents. When the child's upset and angry parents react by scolding or hitting him for stealing, he subconsciously learns that stealing brings him some sort of attention from his parents. An attention-deprived child may unconsciously "prefer" this sort of negative attention to being ignored when he is well-behaved.

Exposure to bad role models

Occasionally, children steal because they have bad role models in their family. There have been rare instances when a child steals because his parent also steals from the shops. Unfortunately in this instance, the child has not been given proper moral messages regarding acceptable social behaviours.

8.2   WHAT SHOULD WE DO WHEN A CHILD STEALS?

When a child is caught doing something wrong, it can be a painful moment for the child and the parent. However, it can be a teachable moment where both parent and child can learn valuable lessons.

Stay Calm

Keep your cool as there is a great temptation to get upset and angry with the child and immediately take out your anger on him. This may lead to potentially dangerous behaviour that can physically harm the child. Additionally, it gives a wrong message to the child that it is acceptable to hit a person who angers you.

Find Out What He Did With The Stolen Money Or Item

This will help you to understand why the child stole. It is important to discover the underlying reason for the child's action so that you can take more effective steps to stop it.

However, it is not easy to get the reason(s) out of the child, especially if you are obviously angry and talk in a threatening tone. By all means, show your displeasure and disapproval of the stealing act, but do keep calm, listen and find out more. If you feel uncomfortable having this discussion with the child, consider getting a trusted adult, like a favourite aunt or school counselor, to talk to the child.

A shy and lonely child, who does not have friends, may steal to obtain presents for others in the hope of winning their friendship. If so, the child needs help to learn how to make and keep friends in more acceptable ways.

A child with low self-esteem may steal to obtain items, such as branded clothes coveted by his peers, in order to gain their attention and approval. This child needs to have his self-esteem raised and be taught better ways to earn peer acceptance. Such a child needs to know that he has to either ask his parents for help to secure the item or save his allowance to get it. You can share with him the pride associated with saving up to buy an item with his own money. He can also learn the important value of living within his means.

Sometimes, stealing is the result of underlying emotional needs or a cry for help or attention. If you discover that this is the reason for the child's stealing, then make attempts to understand and meet the child's needs in more appropriate ways. Sometimes, paying more positive attention to the child may solve the problem. This may include spending time talking to the child, going for a special meal with him or playing his favourite games with him. During this special time with the child, resist the temptation to lecture him about his schoolwork or "bad" behavior. Make it a pleasant experience that the child can look forward to periodically.

Praise the child when you know that he has tried his best and has managed to resist the temptation to steal. For example, if you had left some money on the table and he did not steal it, acknowledge his efforts. Praise the child whenever he is honest in his words and actions. This will encourage him to keep up with his good behaviour.

Let The Child Face The Consequence For His Misbehaviour

This will send a clear message to the child that stealing is not to be tolerated. The consequence meted out to a child depends on the specific situation. Here are some examples:

- If a child has stolen money at home and has not spent it yet, take it back from him. In future, avoid leaving money in the house to avoid any temptation to steal. This is more important in the early stages when the child may not have the motivation to stop stealing or has the desire to stop but his willpower is weak.
- If a child has stolen money but has spent it, make him repay you. You might make him pay a portion of his pocket money every day to you until you have deducted the total amount stolen. Or, you might deduct the amount from his savings in the piggy bank. Whatever you do, give your child a clear message that stealing is painful to others, is unacceptable and has a negative immediate consequence on him.
- If your child has stolen an item from a shop, make him return it to the shop. You might have to personally bring your child to the shop to return the stolen item or pay for it. This is an uneasy, embarrassing

and unpleasant task for both the child and you, the parent. But it is a good opportunity for the child to learn that "my parent disapproves of stealing and will take tough action when I steal" and teaches him the value of being honest.

- You could make the child do an activity that he does not enjoy. This could be writing lines or cleaning the bathroom. He could also be made to miss the weekend family outing that he usually enjoys. You have to explain that the consequences are a result of his stealing so that he can see the connection between a bad deed and its negative consequence.

HELPING A CHILD WHO IS HOT-TEMPERED

It is important to know how to help a hot-tempered child handle his bad temper in an acceptable way. This is part of disciplining him so that he learns to have good social skills in life. A hot-tempered person often struggles with interpersonal relationships. In a fit of rage, the child may injure others or cause damage to property. Some people are hot-tempered most of the time; others may be hot-tempered only when seriously provoked. This depends on one's temperament, personality and upbringing. As good parents, we should teach our children to control their hot temper. It will help them to go a long way.

9.1   WHAT MAKES A HOT-TEMPERED CHILD?

A hot-tempered child may not have learnt to handle his anger and frustrations in a constructive manner. He gets very upset when he cannot get his way, when others do things that upset him (e.g. when another child grabs his toy) or when he cannot achieve what he is trying to do, (e.g. building his Lego car the way he wants to).

For a child with low self-esteem, his anger outbursts may be triggered by situations that attack his self-esteem.

A child may have low levels of tolerance. This level is mainly determined by individual temperaments linked to genetic and inborn traits. Some children are quick to react to situations while others are calmer and remain unfazed in the midst of a trying situation. A child with a difficult temperament will tend to react fast, furiously and impulsively to a difficult situation compared to a child with an easy temperament.

A child may use his temper to get what he wants. This is more likely if he knows, from past experiences, that his parents will give in to his demands when he throws a tantrum. A child may throw bad tantrums if he feels neglected by his parents or caregivers and if his tantrums had drawn their attention in the past.

A child may have learnt to be hot-tempered from others in his life, notably important family figures who tend lose their temper when they are angry.

9.2   DEALING WITH A HOT-TEMPERED CHILD

Remain Calm

Learn to handle your child's anger in a calm and empathic manner. If you lose control yourself, it will be difficult to train your child to handle his angry emotions in a socially acceptable way.

Show Empathy

Let your child know that you understand how he is feeling about what has happened to him. When you see him showing signs of anger, use reflective questions to show that you understand his feelings. You may say, "John, it looks like you are angry with Mei for not lending you her book. Tell me more about it." Let him talk about his angry feelings and about whatever he is upset with. Acknowledge his feelings, even if you feel that the matter is trivial. Give your child a listening ear before you offer advice. That way, he will feel much better and is more likely listen to you.

Teach Ways To Let Out Anger Safely

Direct your child to a quiet place to calm down. You can instruct him to take a few deep breaths and count down from 20 to 0 until his feelings of anger subside. Encourage him to let out his anger by punching a pillow, squeezing a stress ball or going for a run at the park. You can teach your child to engage in coping statements, which are words or sentences that he can say out loud or think in his mind to cope with his anger. For example, he can tell himself, "Alex, calm down, this is not worth getting angry over."

9.3   I HAVE HEARD CHILDREN SWEAR. WHY DO THEY DO IT?

A person usually swears when he is angry, frustrated or wants to hurt those he is upset with. Children often learn to swear from their family members, neighbours or peers. Usually they experiment with the words that they have heard others use. They may try it at school with their peers when they are upset or angry or to show to others that they are "tough" and "part of the group".

Swearing then tends to continue if they receive attention and reactions from others or it gets them what they want. Different families have different standards about the kind of language they allow their children to use. You have to decide what is acceptable and what is taboo in your family.

Here are some rules you can apply to prevent swearing in your family:
- **Decide which words are not acceptable.** Let your child know which words are not to be used at home or outside, and the reasons why they are not allowed.
- **Set a good example.** Children often learn from the adults in their lives. If you do not want a child to swear, do not do so yourself.

- **Explain the rules.** If you hear a child swear, talk to him when both of you are calm. Explain to him why you do not want him to swear and that others would view him negatively if he swears. Suggest alternative words that he can use when he is angry. For example, you can tell him, "Alex, instead of using 'shit', say 'sugar' when you are angry."
- **Provide appropriate praise.** When your child follows your instructions and does not use swear words when he is angry, praise him for that.

9.4   WHAT SHOULD I DO WHEN MY CHILD SWEARS?

Use Planned Ignoring

Planned ignoring is a good method to use the first time you hear a child use a swear word. If your child swears, do not look at him or talk to him. Swearing may stop at this stage, as he gets no reaction from you. If it does not stop, then you have to try other methods.

Teach A Child What To Do

When you hear your child swear, tell him to stop it and teach him what is more acceptable. For example, if your child grabs his brother's toy and swears when he is not allowed to have it, tell him how he should behave instead. Say to him, "Alex, ask your brother nicely if you can have the toy. If he does not give it to you and you are angry, use, 'I'm angry with you' instead of 'you idiot'."

Use Logical Consequences

If your child uses swear words, his friends may not like it and may avoid playing with him. You can tell your child that if he wants his friends to play with him, then he has to stop using swear words. The prospect of losing his friends can be a powerful motivator to stop his swearing behaviour.

CHILD ABUSE

PART 10

So far, we have looked at why we need to discipline a child and how to do it effectively. There is no doubt that effective discipline requires time and effort. Parents naturally love their children. However, there are parents and caregivers who abuse children in their care, tragically causing a premature death, permanent physical disability or emotional and psychological damage.

Sometimes, the abuse is the result of an adult's attempt to discipline a child. It is discipline gone wrong, where ineffective disciplinary methods are used. That is why it is important to understand why child abuse happens, as the line between it and ineffective discipline can be crossed easily. At other times, the abuse is clearly intentional and needs to be investigated and stopped.

10.1 WHAT IS CHILD ABUSE?

Child abuse is defined as a situation where an adult, usually the parent or caregiver, deliberately inflicts physical, emotional or psychological injury on a child. It also includes neglect where the child's basic need for food, clothes, shelter, care and supervision are not adequately provided by the caregiver.

The definition of child abuse differs from culture to culture. What may be considered appropriate in some cultures, like caning a child, may be considered abusive in another culture. In a poor country, the failure of parents to provide adequate care for the child because of poverty may be acceptable and understandable. However, certain behaviours, such as throwing a child against the wall, is considered abuse in almost all cultures.

10.2 WHAT ARE THE TYPES OF CHILD ABUSE?

There are four main types of child abuse:
- Physical abuse (bodily injuries deliberately inflicted on a child).
- Emotional abuse (the use of ridicule, unreasonable criticism and demeaning behaviour that affects the emotional and social well-being and development of a child).
- Sexual abuse (where a child is used to satisfy a deviant adult's sexual needs).
- Neglect (where a child's basic need for food, clothes, shelter, medical care and supervision are not adequately provided for by the caregiver).

10.3 PHYSICAL ABUSE

In order to recognise and prevent child abuse, it is important to know some signs of physical abuse. These include the following:

- Multiple injuries at various stages of healing. There might be old and new bruises, fresh and old cane marks, pinch marks or even cigarette or other burn marks on the body.
- Unexplained injuries on the body. The abuser gives an implausible account of how the injuries were sustained. For example, an abuser who has deliberately cut a child's right index finger may explain that the child, who is right-handed, accidentally cut himself while cutting a fruit.
- Repeated injuries. The abuser gives inconsistent accounts of how the child sustained the injuries.
- Delay in seeking treatment, or no treatment is sought. The abusive parent may fear being caught.
- Behavioural symptoms in the child. Examples include aggression towards others, withdrawal from others, loss of interest in studies and leisure activities due to depression and fear in the presence of the abusive parent.

10.4 EMOTIONAL ABUSE

In emotional abuse, love and emotional care are denied to the child. In addition, the child is consistently humiliated, criticised, shamed or isolated. For example, an unplanned child may be emotionally neglected by his parents and shown that he is not welcome in the family. Emotional abuse does not leave physical scars but can be more damaging to the child than physical abuse.

10.5 SEXUAL ABUSE

A sad reality in life is that children (even infants) and teenagers are sometimes used to satisfy an adult's sexual needs. Most victims of sexual abuse try to keep it a secret and suffer in silence because of shame, embarrassment and fear of the abuser and of not being believed by others around them. Very commonly, the abuser silences the child with threats of harm to the child or his family members. Most cases of child sexual abuse involve a female victim and a male adult known to her (father, stepfather, grandfather, uncle, family friend, neighbour). Sometimes, boys are the victims and adult females are the abusers. Almost all abusers appear normal and are not overtly abusive or inappropriate. Some may even appear to be pleasant and generous with their time and money, in order to gain the trust of their victims and adult caregivers. This is termed "grooming".

Sexual abuse may include the following acts:

- Unwanted and inappropriate fondling of the child's body.
- Getting the child to masturbate the adult.
- Oral, anal or penile-vaginal penetration.
- Exposing the child to pornographic material or adult sexual activity.

The act of sexual abuse might have been an acute traumatic event involving obvious bodily or genital injury, or it could have been a chronic event where the frightened victim is repeatedly abused over a prolonged period. The abuser might touch the child's private parts at first and then gradually engage in more intrusive penetrative sexual acts.

Possible signs of child sexual abuse

- Physical symptoms such as pain and bleeding in the vaginal or penile areas due to injuries or infections, abnormal vaginal discharge, frequency of urination or pain on passing urine or faeces. In some instances, the sexual abuse comes to light only when a girl becomes pregnant as a result of the abuse.
- Emotional changes such as abnormal fears, nightmares, sleep or appetite disturbances, or withdrawn or aggressive behaviour. Some children may lose interest in school and other leisure activities or have crying spells.
- Behavioural changes such as showing age-inappropriate sexualised behaviour towards other children or adults. For example, a 5-year-old sexually abused child might try to insert a doll's leg into the vagina of another classmate in school or she might masturbate frequently and openly or might try to caress her mother's breasts frequently. Some children may even run away from an abusive home and teenagers may engage in sex early or even become promiscuous.

Effects of sexual abuse on the child

When a child is being sexually abused, acute and chronic effects may follow. These effects can be serious and affect the child's emotional, psychological and sexual adjustment and wellbeing. Some of the effects of abuse might appear immediately or shortly after the abuse. Others may appear weeks, months or even years after the sexual assault.

Acute effects include

- abnormal fears,
- crying spells,
- nightmares,
- loss of appetite,
- sleep disturbances,
- anger and irritability,
- aggression,
- acts of self-harm,
- loss of interest in schoolwork.

CASE STUDY

Nine-year-old Hui Ling started to have sleep disturbances at night. She often woke up screaming in the middle of a nightmare. A bright girl, Hui Ling's school grades dropped and she became withdrawn, irritable and fearful of her Uncle Heng. She avoided Uncle Heng whenever he came to the house. Previously, Hui Ling had been an active, bubbly and brave child who adored her uncle and had spent much time alone with him.

When Hui Ling came for treatment, individual time with her was spent to explore gently the issues that were troubling her. Hui Ling drew pictures of a big monster chasing a helpless child and displayed sexualised play (making the dolls touch each other's private parts and doing mouth-to-mouth kissing) with the dolls in a dollhouse. Hui Ling later revealed that her uncle had sexually abused her. Following this disclosure, active steps were taken to protect Hui Ling and gradually, she returned to being a happy and active child.

Chronic effects of child sexual abuse may include depression and low self-esteem as the child may grow up thinking that she is defective and bad because of the abuse. Often, the victim is blamed for the abuse by the abuser, her family and society. Treated like damaged goods, the abused child feels shame and guilt.

Some victims may also

- have difficulty sustaining relationships as they find it hard to trust and relate to others, after having had their trust broken by an important adult in their life,
- become promiscuous or disinterested in others, including members of the opposite sex,
- have sexual difficulties in adulthood such as lack of interest in sex, frigidity or sexual impotence,
- have difficulties parenting their own children, and may even abuse them sexually,
- develop depression and engage in self-harm or suicide attempts,
- develop feelings of self-blame, guilt, low self-esteem,
- develop post-traumatic stress disorder characterised by a state of chronic hyper-arousal and anxiety, sense of foreboding and a doomed future, irritability, aggression, recurrent flashbacks and nightmares, repetitive memories of the abuse, phobic avoidance and sense of panic or anxiety when exposed to people, places or situations that remind her of the abuse, periods of amnesia or "blanking-out",
- develop an eating disorder, multiple personality disorder or borderline personality traits,
- use drug or alcohol to numb their psychological pain and become addicted.

The impact of the sexual abuse depends on factors, such as the chronicity and severity of the abuse, the duration and type of abuse, the child's initial temperamental traits, the level of family functioning before and after the abuse, the family's response to the child's disclosure of abuse, and the nature of the relationship with the abuser. Generally, intra-familial sexual abuse is more damaging as the child feels betrayed by someone who should have provided protection from harm. Sexual acts involving penetration and threats of harm or actual harm is more damaging. Prolonged abuse can make the child feel trapped, helpless, powerless and erode his sense of competence. When the child's family members disbelieve, reject or blame the child for the abuse, the potential impact on the child is worse.

10.6 WHAT CAUSES AN ADULT TO ABUSE A CHILD?
There are three main factors: parental, child, and societal and family factors.

Parental Factors
Generally, parents who abuse their children have a variety of problems. Parents who are at a higher risk of abusing their children are those
- with personality difficulties (antisocial or explosive temper),
- who abuse drugs or alcohol,
- with a mental illness (depression, psychosis or anxiety disorders),
- who themselves had a history of childhood abuse,
- who are stressed (from work or marital problems that make them short-tempered and abusive),
- with unrealistic parental expectations (they turn abusive when their children fail to meet their expectations).

Child Factors
Although it is never acceptable to blame a child for an adult's abusive behaviour, there are certain types of children whose temperament makes them more vulnerable to being abused. Among these are the
- temperamentally difficult child (such a child is often demanding and cries easily),
- the hyperactive child who has conduct problems,
- the mentally or physically handicapped child,
- the child with whom the parents fail to bond (could be due to prolonged separation from the child),
- the shy and timid child.

Societal And Family Factors
When the family does not have a supportive network or has to struggle alone with multiple difficulties, such as poverty, unemployment, overcrowding, marital

strife, parental drug or alcohol abuse or addictions, there is likely to be more stress and abusive care-giving behaviour.

10.7 WHAT CAN PARENTS DO TO PREVENT ABUSE?

As abuse in childhood can lead to harmful short-term and long-term effects, it is important that we detect, help and prevent its occurrence. Parents can prevent abuse in a number of ways.

Use Non-Punitive Disciplinary Factors

Parents should be aware that if they are not careful, they can easily end up abusing their child through the use of ineffective, coercive and punitive disciplinary methods. Parents should learn to discipline their children through the use of non-punitive disciplinary methods. Besides reading books on parenting, parents should also listen to radio and television programmes on the subject and attend parenting talks by child development experts.

Learn To Cope With Their Own Stress

Stressed-out parents can easily turn abusive because of the multiple demands of parenting, looking after one's own elderly parents and work and other domestic problems. Parents should take care of their physical and emotional health as well as the health of their marriage. Parents should seek help early if they cannot cope on their own. There is nothing shameful about getting help from a qualified professional.

Parents should avoid hitting their child in a fit of anger. They should take time-out for themselves if they realise that they are losing control and in danger of hitting their child. Parents should provide unconditional love for their child and remember that he has a voice that needs to be heard and respected, and feelings that can be hurt.

Understand The Stages Of A Child's Development

Parents who are aware of the various stages that children go through are better able to adjust their disciplinary methods and expectations of their child accordingly. These parents are less likely to use harsh disciplinary methods that can hurt their child.

Teach Your Child How To Protect Himself From Abuse

To prevent sexual abuse, you can teach your child to distinguish between:
- good touches, like a handshake, that they can receive,
- bad touches that they should avoid. One example of a bad touch is fondling of the child's private parts.

Teach your child what to do when he or she receives a bad touch. For instance, let your child know that she should let a trusted adult know about the inappropriate behavior at once, even if the abuser had warned them not to. Teach your child to avoid going out with a stranger. However, quite a number of children, who had been taught about good and bad touches, feel helpless and keep quiet when faced with an abusive situation. The power difference between the abusive adult and child, the sense of shame and helplessness, and threats from the abuser can easily intimidate and silence the child.

As a parent, do not leave your child with a caregiver you do not know well. If your child refuses to visit someone and cries when forced to visit that person, check for any possible abuse and take protective action if needed. Never brush off complaints of abuse as a lie or a figment of the child's imagination.

Although abuse in childhood increases the likelihood of a victim growing up to be an abusive adult, there are many cases where the victim becomes a survivor and grows up into a non-abusive and well-adjusted adult.

10.8 CHILD NEGLECT

Child neglect refers to a parent's or caregiver's failure to provide a child with food, clothing, shelter, safety, supervision and medical care despite the parent's or caregiver's ability and means to do so. As a result, the child might die or suffer from impaired physical, emotional or social development and even permanent disability. In fact, child neglect is more common than child abuse and is an important cause of child morbidity and mortality. The neglect may be physical, educational, or emotional in nature.

Physical Neglect

Physical neglect refers to the caregiver's failure to provide the child with basic physical needs, such as safe, clean and adequate food, clothing, shelter and medical care. Physically neglected children may be chronically smelly or dirty, lack suitable clothing, have untreated medical or dental conditions, appear thin and malnourished, have poor weight or height gain, repeated injuries from poor adult supervision and delayed physical milestones such as poor language skills and delayed walking. Some neglected children may be abandoned by their parents, left unsupervised alone at home or allowed to publicly beg for their needs.

Emotional neglect

Emotional neglect refers to the caregiver's failure to provide the child with love, warmth, nurturance, encouragement, supervision and support. Such a child may end up emotional problems, poor social skills and even poor physical growth and development.

Educational neglect

Educational neglect refers to a caregiver's failure to provide the child with appropriate educational opportunities for the child. Children whose educational needs are neglected are often not enrolled in a suitable school or allowed to chronically be absent from school without a valid reason.

WHERE CAN I GO FOR HELP?

PART 11

Nowadays, in nearly all countries, child maltreatment is considered a criminal act and there are governmental and non-governmental agencies that actively strive to protect children from abuse. These agencies act as advocates to promote the child's well-being and work with parents or caregivers who need guidance, support and practical assistance in parenting matters.

In Singapore, child abuse is considered a criminal act and the abuser can be prosecuted in court. The Ministry of Social and Family Development (MSF) in Singapore is responsible for the welfare and protection of children in Singapore. It investigates complaints of child abuse and has the authority to take appropriate action, including temporary removal of the abused child to a place of safety and making a police report.

The Ministry places a child suspected of being abused under the supervision of its welfare officers and works closely with the offending parent or caregiver and the non-offending parent or caregiver to prevent further abuse. Where the abuse is serious and there is little prospect of change in the parents (who are usually having serious problems themselves), the child is removed to a welfare home or foster care for a few years, until the child is older and capable of protecting himself. The child is also provided with counselling to help him deal with the after effects of abuse.

PLACES WHERE PARENTS AND CHILDREN CAN GET HELP:

SINGAPORE
Child Guidance Clinic
Health Promotion Board Building
3 Second Hospital Avenue, #03–01, Singapore 168937
Tel: 6435 3878 / 6435 3879

Child Protection and Welfare Services
SLF Podium, 512A Thomson Road, #01–01 to#01–09, Singapore 298137
Tel: 1800 777 0000

Counselling and Care Centre
Block 536, Upper Cross Street, #05–241, Hong Lim Complex. Singapore 050536
Tel: 6536 6366

Association of Muslim Professionals (AMP)
AMP @ Pasir Ris, 1 Pasir Ris Drive 4, #05–11, Singapore 519 457
Tel: 6416 3966 (Main Line)
     6416 3963 (Social Services Division)
     6416 3960 (Help Line)

MALAYSIA
Jabatan Kebajikan Masyarakat
Aras 6, 9-18. No 55, Persiaran Perdana, Presint 4, 62100 Putrajaya
Tel: 03 8000 8000

HONG KONG
Social Welfare Department
8/F Wu Ching House, 213 Queen's Road, East Wanchai, Hong Kong
Hotline: (852) 2343 2255

THAILAND
The Center for the Protection of Children's Rights Foundation (CPCR)
979 Charansanitwong 12 Road, Wat Tha Phra, Bangkokokyai, Bangkok 10600,
Thailand
Tel: 66 2 412 1196

INDONESIA
National Commission for Child Protection/Komisi Nasional Perlindungan Anak (NCCP)
Jalan TB Simatupang 33, Jakarta, DKI Jakarta, Indonesia
Tel: 021 840 0573

ENGLAND
The National Society for the Prevention of Cruelty to Children (NSPCC)
Weston House, 42 Curtain Road, London EC2A 3NH
Tel: 0844 892 1026

AUSTRALIA
New South Wales: **Department of Family & Community Services**
Tel: 132 111

Victoria: **Department of Health and Human Services**
Tel: 131 278 (after-hours emergency)

Queensland: **Department of Communities, Child Safety and Disability Services**
Tel: (07) 3235 9999 or 1800 177 135 (after-hours and weekends)

Western Australia: **Department for Child Protection**
Tel: 1800 622 258 or (08) 9223 1111 / 1800 199 008 (after-hours)

South Australia: **Department for Education and Child Development**
Tel: 131 478

Tasmania: **Department of Health and Human Services**
Tel: 1300 737 639

Australian Capital Territory: **Community Services Directorate**
Tel: 1300 556 729

Northern Territory: **Office of Children and Families**
Tel: 1800 700 250

UNITED STATES
Childhelp
Hotline: 1800 422 4453

If in doubt, do not hesitate to make an enquiry at the nearest Neighbourhood Police Post or Police Divisional Headquarters.

USEFUL RESOURCES

Books

ADHD: How to Deal with Very Difficult Children: Alan Train. Souvenir Press (1996)

Confident Parenting: A Hands-on Approach to Children: Anne Davis. Souvenir Press (1997)

Help Your Child to Cope: Cai Yiming & Daniel Fung. Times Books International (1998)

When Parents Love Too Much: Laurie Ashner & Mitch Meyerson. William Morrow & Company, Inc (1997)

Websites

American Academy of Child & Adolescent Psychiatry
www.aacap.org/aacap/Families_and_Youth/Facts_for_Families/Home.aspx

Child and Youth Health
www.cyh.com

ABOUT THE AUTHORS

Dr Parvathy Pathy

Dr Parvathy Pathy is a Senior Consultant Psychiatrist attached to the Child Guidance Clinic at the Institute of Mental Health. She has been practicing medicine since she graduated from the National University of Singapore in 1983 and qualified as a psychiatrist in 1990. She received further training in the area of child abuse and juvenile offending at the Royal Children's Hospital, in Melbourne, Australia, and from the Young Abusers Project in London.

Dr Parvathy sees and counsels children, teenagers and their families who come to her with a wide range of emotional, psychological and behavioural problems. She is interested in children's and women's issues. In 2002, Dr Pathy wrote *Kim's Story*, a short story about unconditional love and adoption for the Institute of Mental Health.

Ms Fiona Tan

Ms Fiona Tan is a Senior Clinical Psychologist attached to the Child Guidance Clinic at the Institute of Mental Health. She earned her Honours Degree in Psychology and Crime and Deviance from the University of Toronto. Following her graduation, she worked as an Intake Counselor at Family Transition Place, a women's shelter in Orangeville, Ontario where she counselled adolescent and adult survivors of domestic violence and sexual assaults.

After returning to Singapore in 2007, Ms Tan obtained her Master's Degree in Clinical Psychology at the National University of Singapore. She currently provides assessments and therapeutic interventions for children and adolescents who struggle with anxiety or mood difficulties as well as trauma and offending issues. She is especially interested in working with survivors of traumatic events.

Mr Shyon Loo

Mr Shyon Loo is a Senior Clinical Psychologist under the Department of Child and Adolescent Psychiatry at the Institute of Mental Health (IMH). He holds a Master's degree in Clinical Psychology and Certificate in Advanced Studies in Counseling from the Loyola University in Maryland. He worked at the University of Maryland and the Johns Hopkins University in the US before joining the Department of Child and Adolescent Psychiatry at IMH. He currently provides assessments and therapeutic interventions for young persons with inappropriate sexualised behaviour, young offenders, victims of trauma and youths at risk of offending.